Hawaiian

Marcy Schaaf

The Great Egg-scape:

He ʻAi Moku Moʻa - Māhele 2

Marcy Schaaf

The Great Egg-scape:

A Chicken Island Adventure - Part 2

Welcome back to Chicken Island, where feathers fly and adventures abound! In this egg-citing sequel to "The Chicken Island Adventure," our plucky poultry pals find themselves in a feathery frenzy like never before. When the chickens catch a case of Brodie Fever and decide they'd rather be mamas than egg layers, it's up to Farmer Fred and his clever companions to hatch a plan to get them back on track. Join us as we embark on a journey filled with laughter, friendship, and plenty of egg-squisite surprises. So grab your feathers and get ready to cluck along because the fun is just beginning on Chicken Island!

Welina mai i ka mokupuni ʻo Chicken, kahi e lele ai nā hulu a nui nā mea hoʻokipa! I loko o kēia ʻōlelo hua manu i ka "The Chicken Island Adventure," ʻike kā mākou mau hoa moa ʻohi i loko o ka hulu manu e like me ka wā ma mua. Ke loaʻa nā moa i kahi hihia o Brodie Fever a hoʻoholo e makemake lākou e lilo i mau mama ma mua o nā papa hua manu, aia iā Farmer Fred a me kāna mau hoa akamai e hana i kahi hoʻolālā e hoʻihoʻi iā lākou i ke ala. E hui pū me mākou i ka huakaʻi i piha i ka ʻakaʻaka, ka hoaloha, a me ka nui o nā mea haohao hua manu. No laila, e hopu i kou mau hulu a e hoʻomākaukau i ka cluck no ka mea ke hoʻomaka nei ka leʻaleʻa ma Chicken Island!

The Great Egg-scape:
A Chicken Island Adventure
- Part 2

Once upon a time, on Chicken Island, feathers were about to ruffle in the most egg-squisite way!

I kekahi manawa, ma ka Mokupuni ʻo Chicken, ua kokoke e haʻalulu nā hulu ma ke ʻano hua manu!

The chickens were acting more scrambled than sunny-side up! Instead of laying eggs, they were nesting...

Ua ʻoi aku ka maikaʻi o nā moa ma mua o ka ʻaoʻao o ka lā! Ma kahi o ka waiho ʻana i nā hua, ua pūnana lākou...

"What's going on?" exclaimed Farmer Fred, his eyebrows raised.

"He aha ka mea e hana nei?" i hoʻōho ai ʻo Farmer Fred, ua piʻi aʻe kona mau kuʻemaka.

"We've got a case of Brodie Fever!" announced Henrietta, clutching a sunflower seed like it was her firstborn..

"Ua loaʻa iā mākou kahi hihia o Brodie Fever!" i hoʻolaha aku ai ʻo Henrietta, e hoʻopaʻa ana i kahi hua pua lā e like me kāna hiapo.

"Brodie Fever? Is that contagious?" asked Farmer Fred, backing away cautiously.

"Brodie Fever? He lele anei ia?" i ninau aku ai ka Mahiai Fred, me ke akahele.

The rooster with a beak for brains, strutted forward. "Oh, it's spreading faster than gossip at a coop party!"

ʻO ka moa me ka nuku no ka lolo, hele i mua. "ʻAe, ʻoi aku ka wikiwiki o ka laha ʻana ma mua o ka ʻōlelo ʻōhumu ma kahi pāʻina coop!"

"But we need eggs for breakfast, lunch, and dinner!" fretted Farmer Fred, his stomach growling in protest..

"Akā, pono mākou i nā hua no ka ʻaina kakahiaka, ka ʻaina awakea, a me ka ʻaina ahiahi!" Huhū ʻo Farmer Fred, uwē kona ʻōpū i ke kūʻē.

"Don't crack up just yet, Farmer Fred! We've got this!" chirped Cheddar.

"Mai ʻoki wale ʻoe, e Farmer Fred! Loaʻa iā mākou kēia!" kani ʻo Cheddar.

The chickens huddled together in the coop,

brainstorming like a bunch of brainy birds..

Hui pu ka moa i ka hale,

ka noʻonoʻo ʻana e like me ka pūʻulu o nā manu lolo.

"We need a coop-tastrophe to distract them!" suggested Daisy, twirling a dandelion in her beak.

"Pono mākou i kahi coop-tastrophe e ho'ohuli iā lākou!" wahi a Daisy, e wiliwili ana i ka dandelion ma kona nuku.

"Like a hen-sized disco ball!" clucked Fluffy, her feathers practically disco dancing with excitement.

"E like me ka kinipōpō disco ka nui o ka moa!" u'i 'o Fluffy, 'o kona mau hulu e hula disco me ka hau'oli.

"We could give them egg-laying lessons!" proposed Pecky, doing her best impression of a professor with a beak.

"Hiki iā mākou ke hāʻawi iā lākou i nā haʻawina hoʻohua hua!" i noi aku ai ʻo Pecky, e hana ana i kona manaʻo maikaʻi loa i kahi polopeka me ka nuku.

"And a fashion show with the fanciest eggshell hats!" added Cluckington, posing dramatically with an imaginary runway.

"A he hō‘ike‘ike ki‘i me nā pāpale hulu hua manu maika‘i loa!" i ho‘ohui ‘ia ‘o Cluckington, me ke ‘ano nui me ke ala holo no‘ono‘o.

The chickens nodded in agreement, their beaks bobbing like they were agreeing with the world's funniest joke..

Kunu mai la na moa me ka ae like me ka nuku o ko lakou nuku me he mea la e ae ana lakou i ka hoohenehene o ka honua.

They worked faster than a chicken with a vendetta against a worm, preparing for the grand distraction.

Ua ʻoi aku ka wikiwiki o kā lākou hana ma mua o ka moa me ka hoʻopaʻapaʻa kūʻē i kahi ilo, e hoʻomākaukau ana no ka hoʻohilahila nui.

When the big day arrived, Chicken Island turned into a coop-tastic carnival of clucks and chuckles.

I ka hōʻea ʻana mai o ka lā nui, ua lilo ʻo Chicken Island i kahi carnival coop-tastic of clucks and chuckles.

The chickens rolled eggs like they were competing for the Egg Olympics, aiming for the gold medal in egg rolling.

ʻOlokaʻa ʻia nā hua manu e like me ka hoʻokūkū ʻana no ka ʻOlumepika Egg, e ʻimi ana i ka mekala gula ma ka ʻōwili hua.

They danced like nobody was watching, except everybody was watching, so they danced even harder!

Hula lākou me he mea lā ʻaʻohe kanaka e nānā ana, koe naʻe nā kānaka a pau e nānā ana, no laila ua ʻoi aku ka ikaika o kā lākou hula!

Even Farmer Fred got in on the action,
doing the chicken dance with a fervor that
would make any chicken proud !

Ua komo pū ʻo Farmer Fred i ka hana, e hana ana i ka hulahula moa me ka ikaika e hoʻokiʻekiʻe ai kekahi moa!

The distractions worked like magic! The broody chickens forgot all about being mamas and became egg-straordinary egg layers once more.

Ua hana like nā mea hoʻowalewale! Ua poina nā moa broody i ka lilo ʻana i mau mama a ua lilo hou i mau ʻano hua manu.

"Thank you, thank you very much!" Farmer Fred exclaimed, his heart as warm as a freshly laid egg.

"Mahalo, mahalo nui loa!" Ua hoʻōho ʻo Freder, ʻo kona puʻuwai me he huamoa i hoʻomoe hou ʻia.

"Who needs Hollywood when you've got Chicken Island?" chuckled Cheddar, leading a conga line around the coop.

"ʻO wai ka mea e pono ai iā Hollywood ke loaʻa iā ʻoe ʻo Chicken Island?" ʻakaʻaka ʻo Cheddar, e alakaʻi ana i kahi laina conga a puni ka coop.

From that day on, Chicken Island was filled with laughter, eggs, and happy clucks, like a permanent party for poultry.

Mai ia lā mai, ua hoʻopiha ʻia ʻo Chicken Island i ka ʻakaʻaka, nā hua manu, a me nā ʻaka hauʻoli, e like me ka pāʻina mau no ka moa.

And whenever a chicken felt broody, they knew just what to do—shake their tail feathers and join the fun!

A i kēlā me kēia manawa i manaʻo ʻia ka moa, ʻike pono lākou i ka mea e hana ai - lulu i ko lākou hulu huelo a hui pū i ka leʻaleʻa!

But wait, the end? Not even close! There are more adventures waiting to be hatched on Chicken Island.

Akā e kali, ka hopena? ʻAʻole kokoke loa! Nui aʻe nā huakaʻi e kali ana e hoʻopaʻa ʻia ma Chicken Island.

So grab your feathers, hold onto your beak, and get ready for another egg-stravaganza!

No laila e hopu i kou hulu, e pa'a i kou nuku, a e ho'omākaukau no kahi hua manu-stravaganza hou!

And remember, there's no problem too scrambled that a little laughter can't unscramble.

A e hoʻomanaʻo, ʻaʻohe pilikia i hiki ʻole i ka ʻakaʻaka ke wehe.

The end...

or is it just the beginning of another egg-stravaganza?

Ka hopena...

a i ʻole he hoʻomaka wale nō ia o kekahi hua manu-stravaganza?

Glossary:

Brodie:

A condition where chickens become broody, meaning they want to sit on eggs to hatch them and become mothers.

Egg-squisite:

used to describe something that is exceptionally beautiful, delightful, or finely crafted in relation to eggs. It's a whimsical way to express admiration or appreciation for the quality or appeal of eggs, whether in appearance, taste, or any other aspect.

Egg-straordinary:

It's used to describe something that is exceptionally remarkable, or impressive in a context related to eggs or chickens. In the context of the story, it emphasizes the uniqueness and special qualities of the chickens' egg-related adventures and antics..

Egg-stravaganza:

It refers to a lively and extravagant event or celebration centered around eggs or poultry-related activities. In the context of the story, it emphasizes the exciting and festive nature of the chickens' adventures and the fun-filled activities they partake in, such as egg rolling, dancing, and more..

Egg-citing:

It describes something that is thrilling, enjoyable, or filled with anticipation, particularly in relation to eggs or chicken-related activities. In the context of the story, it emphasizes the excitement and adventure that the chickens experience as they embark on their egg-related escapades.

Egg-ceptional:

It refers to something that is outstanding, extraordinary, or remarkable, particularly in the context of eggs or chicken-related matters. In the story, "egg-ceptional" underscores the remarkable and special qualities of the chickens' adventures and the creative solutions they come up with to overcome challenges.

The actual chickens this story's about!

Books By Schaaf

www.BookBySchaaf.com

Find us at:

www.ingramcontent.com/pod-product-compliance
Lightning Source LLC
LaVergne TN
LVHW082252150826
845677LV00009B/1614
* 9 7 9 8 3 3 0 2 1 6 8 8 8 *

You need to be able to compare and contrast the particular advantages and disadvantages of using different types of telescopes on Earth and in space to make observations of, and deductions about, the Universe.

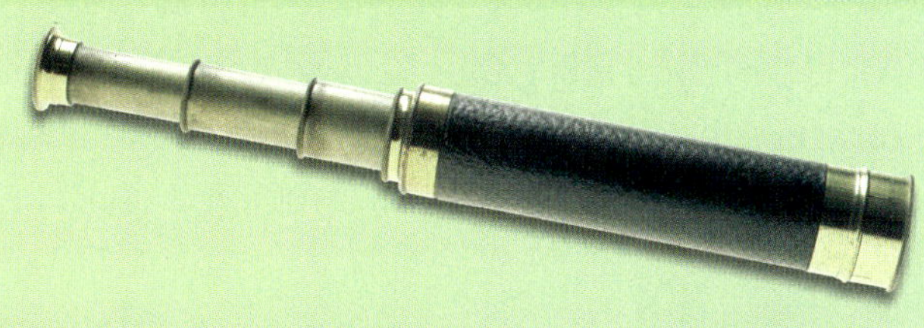

Astronomy News, Star Charts, Space Pictures

http:// www.outerspace.co.uk/asy/default.aspx

Apple .Mac Amazon eBay Yahoo! News ▾

ABOUT ASTRONOMY

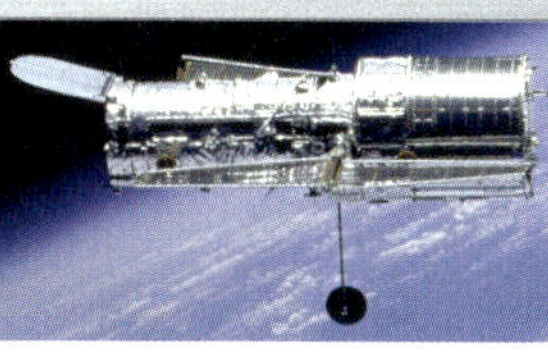

ASTRO FOR KIDS
THE STARRY SKY
THE SUN
MOONS AND PLANETS
METEORS
COMETS
THE AURORA
USING BINOCULARS
TELESCOPES
ABOUT
HOW TO USE
PHOTOGRAPHY

The main types of telescope used to observe the Universe from Earth are reflecting telescopes, refracting telescopes and radio telescopes.

Type	Advantages	Disadvantages
Reflecting Telescope	• Cheap. • Accurate colour representation.	• Limited to visible light. • Need cleaning and realigning frequently. • Poorer image quality than refracting telescope. • Produce inverted (upside down) images. • Bulky compared to refracting telescopes of same strength. • Can only be used at night.
Refracting Telescope	• Produce sharp, detailed images. • Portable. • Easy to maintain.	• Limited to visible light. • Images have a halo of false colours around them. • More expensive than reflecting telescopes. • Produce inverted images. • Can only be used at night.
Radio Telescope	• Unaffected by light so can be used 24 hours a day. • Can be used to accurately map the Universe. • Detect emissions of gas between stars that are not visible to the human eye.	• Require massive / multiple antennas. • Require a large, permanent site. • Very expensive to set up.

The Hubble Space Telescope belongs to a family of optical telescopes called catadioptrics. They use both mirrors and lenses to overcome a lot of the disadvantages associated with reflecting and refracting telescopes. They produce sharp, detailed images with accurate colours and they are smaller than reflectors and cheaper than refractors of the same strength.

In 1990, NASA went to great expense and risk to launch the Hubble Space Telescope. Within weeks of the launch, it became apparent that there were serious problems with the optical system. Although the first images appeared to be sharper than ground-based images, the telescope failed to achieve a final sharp focus. The problem was found to be a wrongly shaped mirror, which was replaced in 1993. Since then, the telescope has been visited regularly for servicing and updates. These visits are costly processes.

So, what are the advantages to science of having an optical telescope in space?

Optical Telescope in Space	Optical Telescope on Earth
Advantages • Can be used 24 hours a day. • Clear pictures as no light pollution, clouds or storms. **Disadvantages** • Very expensive to build, put up and maintain / repair. • Cannot focus on near objects.	**Advantages** • Cheaper to build, service and repair. **Disadvantages** • Can only be used at night and if skies are clear. • Has to be placed in a remote position due to light pollution.

Example Questions

For Unit 1, you will either have to complete two objective tests (matching and multiple choice questions) or one written paper (longer, structured questions).

1 Every year large amounts of heat energy are lost from our homes.

Reducing this energy loss helps to cut energy bills and save money.

Which of these methods would not help to reduce heat loss from the home?

A Installing double glazing. ☐

B Installing a fire guard. ☑

C Fitting roof insulation. ☐

D Fitting draught excluders. ☐ *(1 mark)*

1

2 Gamma rays can be hazardous to humans.

Which statement describes why they are dangerous?

A Gamma rays can penetrate the body and be absorbed by organs. ☑

B Gamma rays kill cancer cells. ☐

C Gamma rays cannot pass through paper. ☐

D Gamma rays cannot get out of the body. ☐ *(1 mark)*

1

3 a) What causes a turbine in a fossil fuel power station to turn?

Fuel is burnt to heat water, producing steam which turns the turbine.

(1 mark)

b) Two resources that can be used to generate electricity are nuclear fuel and wind. In the table below, give one advantage and one disadvantage for each resource used to generate electricity.

Nuclear Fuel	**Wind**
Advantage	**Advantage**
Flexible in meeting demand.	No pollutant gases produced.
Disadvantage	**Disadvantage**
Produces radioactive waste.	Produces small amounts of electricity.

(4 marks)

3

1. Read the question carefully. If you missed the word 'not' you would get this simple question wrong!
2. If you are unsure about the answer to a multiple-choice question, eliminate the options that are obviously wrong or not relevant to the question first.
3. The amount of space and number of marks available is a clue to how much information you need to provide. This question requires a short, succinct answer.
4. Make sure you answer all the questions in full. This question requires four responses in total (an advantage and a disadvantage for two different methods).
5. Where there are several possible answers, choose one that you are certain is correct.

Key Words

Atom – the smallest part of an element that displays the chemical properties of the element

Conductor – a substance that readily transfers heat or energy

Current – the flow of electric charge through a conductor

Efficiency – the ratio of energy output to energy input, expressed as a percentage

Energy – the ability to do work, measured in joules

Half-life – the time taken for half the atoms in radioactive material to decay

Ions – a charged particle formed when an atom gains or loses electrons

Isotope – atoms of the same element but with a different number of neutrons

Kilowatt – a unit for measuring power, equal to 1000 watts

Kilowatt hour – the amount of electrical energy used by a 1 kilowatt device in 1 hour

Non-renewable – energy sources that cannot be replaced in a lifetime

Power – the rate of doing work, measured in watts

Reflection – a wave (e.g. light or sound) that is thrown back from a surface

Refraction – the change in direction of a wave as it passes from one medium to another

Renewable – energy sources that can be replaced

Telescope – a device that magnifies distant images

Thermal energy – heat energy

Transfer – to move energy from one place to another

Transform – to change energy from one form into another, e.g. electrical energy to heat energy

Transformer – an electrical device used to change the voltage of alternating currents

Transmission – the sending of information or electricity over a communications line or a circuit

Voltage – potential difference, expressed in volts

Unit 2

12.1

How can we describe the way things move?

Movement is not easy to describe. Objects can move at different speeds and in different directions. Distance–time graphs and velocity–time graphs can help to describe movement. To understand this, you need to know…

- what speed, acceleration and velocity are
- how to calculate acceleration
- how a distance–time graph represents speed
- how a velocity–time graph represents acceleration and distance travelled.

Speed

One way of describing the movement of an object is by measuring its **speed**, i.e. how fast it is moving. Since this cyclist travels a distance of 8 metres every 1 second we can say that the speed of the cyclist is 8 metres per second (m/s).

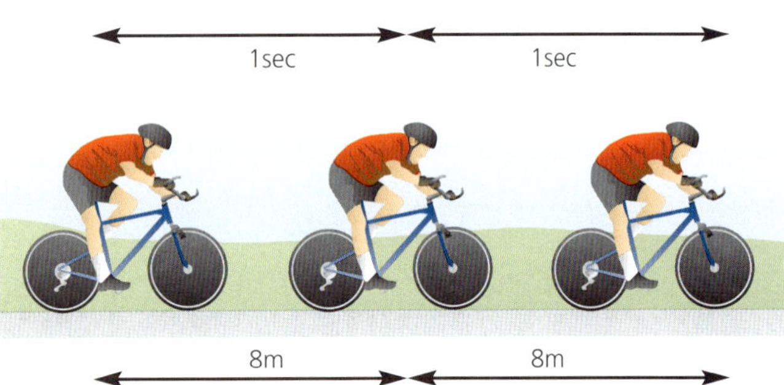

If we want to work out the speed of any moving object we need to know two things:

- the distance it travels
- the time it takes to travel that distance.

We can then calculate the speed of the object using the following formula…

$$\text{Speed (m/s)} = \frac{\text{Distance travelled (m)}}{\text{Time taken (s)}}$$

$$\frac{d}{s \times t}$$

Speed can also be measured in kilometres per hour (km/h) and miles per hour (mph).

Example

Calculate the speed of a cyclist who travels 2400m in 5 minutes.

$$\text{Speed (m/s)} = \frac{\text{Distance travelled (m)}}{\text{Time taken (s)}} = \frac{2400}{300} = \mathbf{8m/s}$$

Multiply 5 minutes by 60 to get time in seconds

Distance–Time Graphs

The slope of a **distance–time graph** represents the speed of an object; the steeper the slope, the greater the speed.

Stationary object: 'y' axis shows distance from a fixed point (0), not total distance travelled.

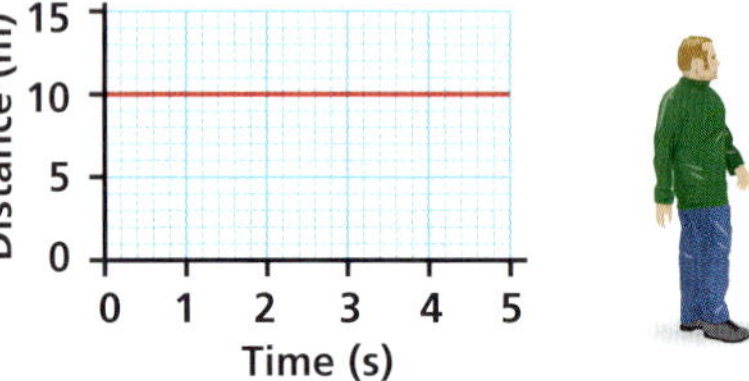

Object is moving at a constant speed of 2m/s.

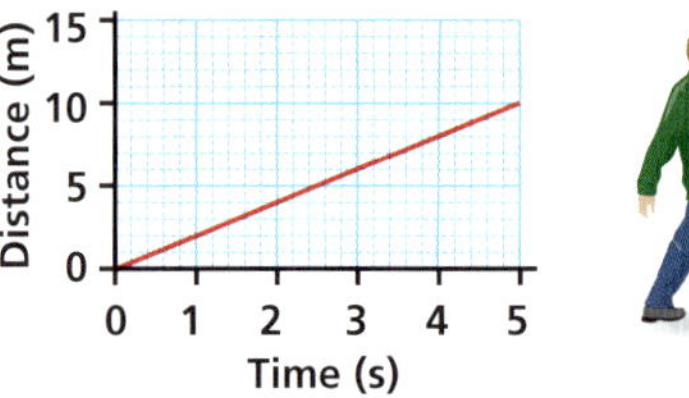

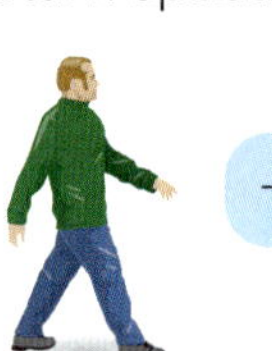

$\frac{10}{5}$ = **2m/s**

Object is moving at a greater constant speed of 3m/s.

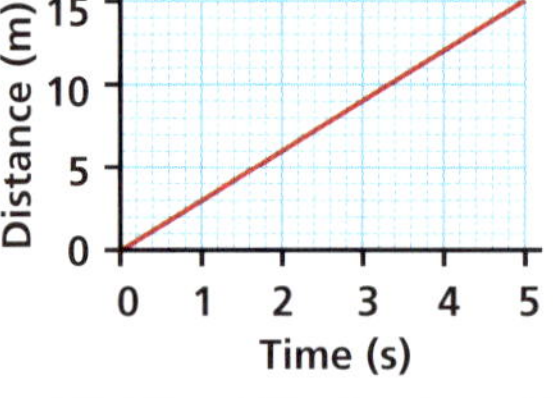

$\frac{15}{5}$ = **3m/s**

Velocity

Velocity and speed are not the same thing. The velocity of a moving object describes its speed in a given direction, i.e. the speed and the direction of travel are both known.

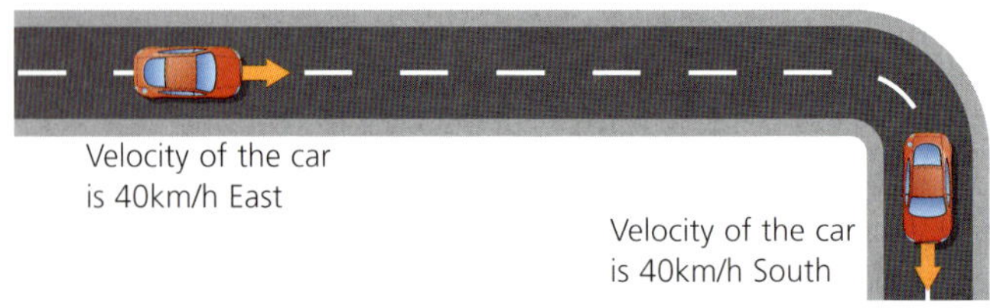

Acceleration

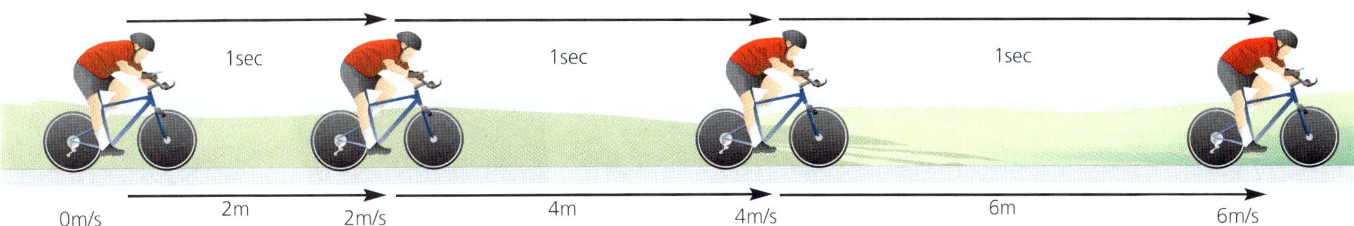

The **acceleration** of an object is the rate at which its velocity changes. In other words it is a measure of how quickly an object speeds up or slows down.

The cyclist above increases his velocity by 2 metres per second every second. So, we can say that his acceleration is $2m/s^2$ (2 metres per second, per second). To work out the acceleration of any moving object you need to know two things:

- the change in velocity
- the time taken for this change in velocity.

You can then calculate the speed of the object using the following formula...

$$\text{Acceleration } (m/s^2) \text{ (or deceleration)} = \frac{\text{Change in velocity (m/s)}}{\text{Time taken for change (s)}}$$

where v is the final velocity and u is the starting velocity

$$\frac{(v - u)}{a \times t}$$

There are two important points to be aware of:

1. the cyclist above increases his velocity by the *same amount* every second; the *actual* distance travelled each second increases
2. deceleration is simply a negative acceleration, i.e. it describes an object that is slowing down.

Example

A cyclist accelerates uniformly from rest and reaches a velocity of 10m/s after 5s, then decelerates uniformly and comes to a halt in a further 10s. Calculate **a)** his acceleration, and **b)** his deceleration.

a) Acceleration $= \dfrac{\text{Change in velocity}}{\text{Time taken}} = \dfrac{10 - 0}{5} = \mathbf{2m/s^2}$

b) Deceleration $= \dfrac{\text{Change in velocity}}{\text{Time taken}} = \dfrac{0 - 10}{10} = \mathbf{1m/s^2}$

i.e. a deceleration (make sure you state this)

Velocity–Time Graphs

The slope of a **velocity–time graph** represents the acceleration of the object; the steeper the slope, the greater the acceleration. The area underneath the line in a velocity–time graph represents the total distance travelled.

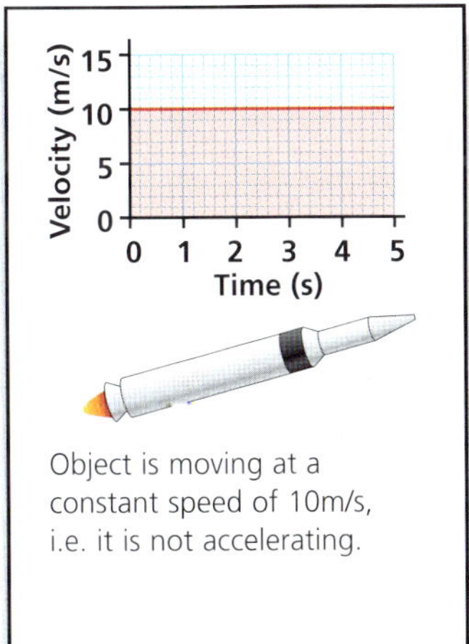

Object is moving at a constant speed of 10m/s, i.e. it is not accelerating.

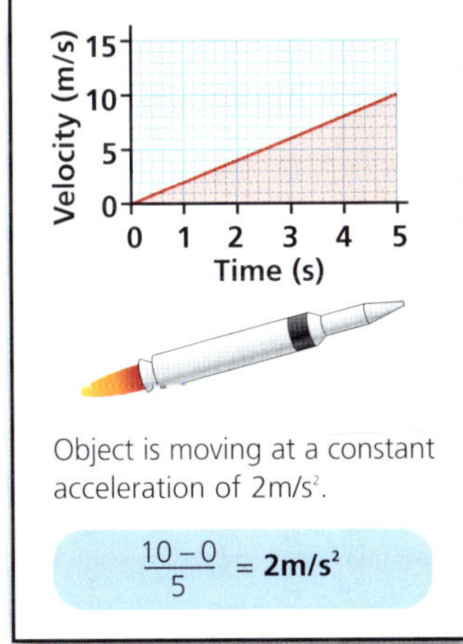

Object is moving at a constant acceleration of $2m/s^2$.

$\frac{10-0}{5} = \mathbf{2m/s^2}$

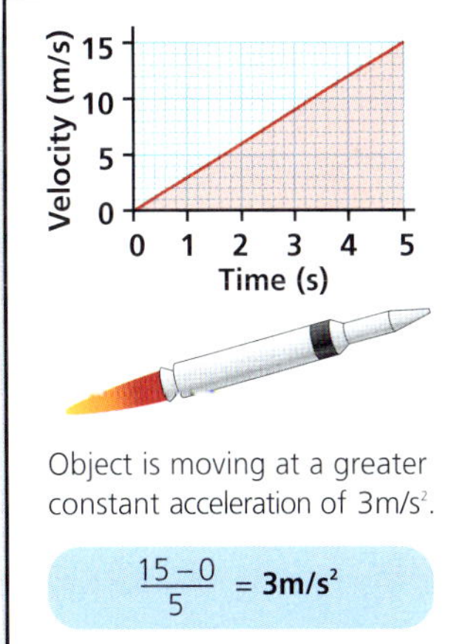

Object is moving at a greater constant acceleration of $3m/s^2$.

$\frac{15-0}{5} = \mathbf{3m/s^2}$

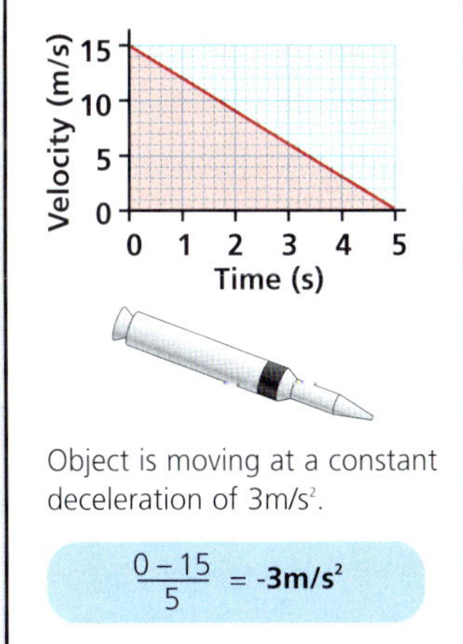

Object is moving at a constant deceleration of $3m/s^2$.

$\frac{0-15}{5} = \mathbf{-3m/s^2}$

How Science Works

You need to be able to construct distance–time graphs for a body moving in a straight line when the body is stationary or moving with constant speed.

Example

An athlete is training for a marathon. She runs at a constant speed for 1 minute and then rests for 20 seconds to allow her pulse rate to slow down. She repeats this 4 times. For each minute that she is running, she covers 400m. This information can be plotted on a distance–time graph (see below).

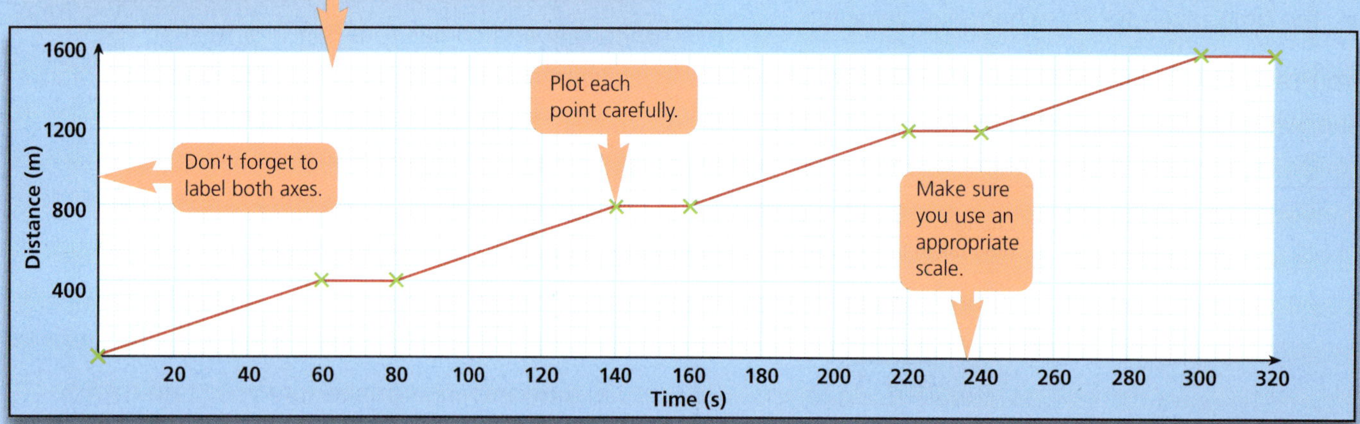

You need to be able to construct velocity–time graphs for a body moving with a constant velocity or a constant acceleration.

Example

The same athlete practises a sprint finish by running in a straight line at a constant speed (i.e. velocity) of 7m/s for 20 seconds before gradually increasing her speed to a sprint. It takes her 20 seconds to reach a top speed of 9m/s accelerating at a constant rate. She then maintains this top speed for a further 20 seconds. This information can be plotted on a velocity–time graph (see opposite).

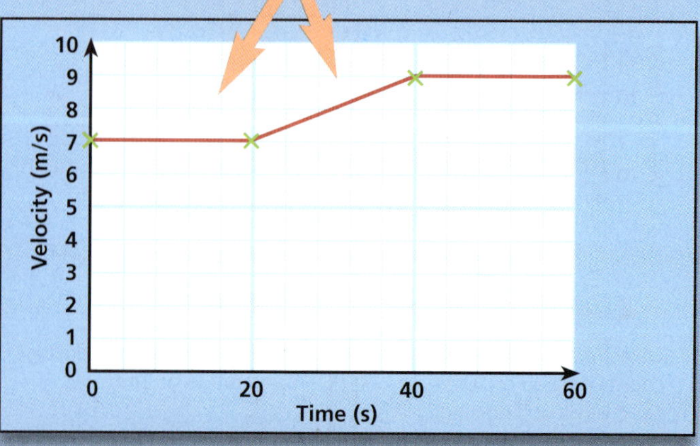

HT

You need to be able to calculate the speed of a body from the slope of a distance–time graph.

Example

Here is a distance–time graph. Calculate the speed of the body during the three parts of the journey using the formula...

$$\text{Speed} = \frac{\text{Distance travelled}}{\text{Time taken}}$$

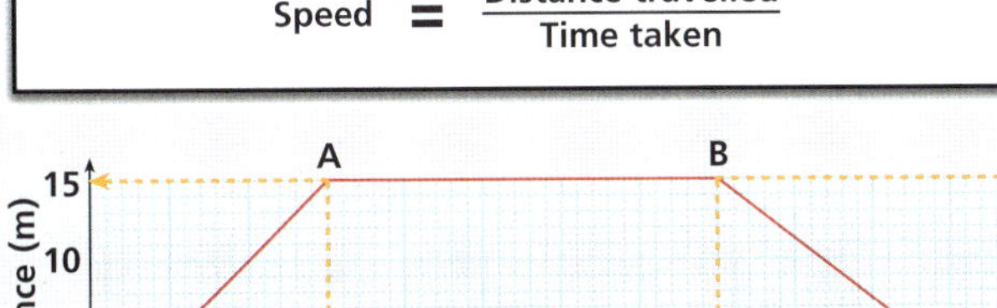

0 to A: Substitute figures into the formula...

Speed from 0 to A = $\frac{15\text{m}}{3\text{s}}$ = **5m/s**

A to B: Object stationary (no slope). Prove this using the formula...

Speed from A to B = $\frac{0\text{m}}{5\text{s}}$ = **0m/s**

B to C: Substitute figures into the formula...

Speed from B to C = $\frac{15\text{m}}{4\text{s}}$ = **3.75m/s**

So, the object travelled at 5m/s for 3 seconds, remained stationary for 5 seconds then travelled at 3.75m/s for 4 seconds back to the starting point.

You need to be able to calculate the acceleration of a body from the slope of a velocity–time graph and the distance travelled from a velocity–time graph.

Example

Here is a velocity–time graph. Calculate the acceleration of the three parts of the journey and the total distance travelled.

$$\text{Acceleration} = \frac{\text{Change in velocity}}{\text{Time taken}}$$

Total distance travelled = Total area under graph

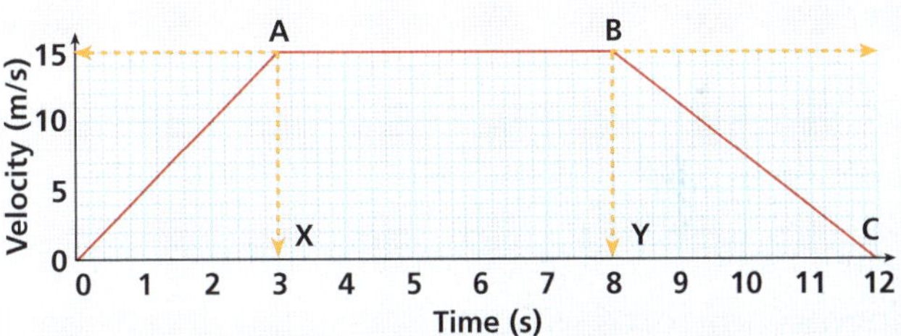

0 to A: Substitute figures into the formula...

Acceleration from 0 to A = $\frac{15\text{m/s}}{3\text{s}}$ = **5m/s²**

A to B: Constant velocity (no slope = no acceleration). Prove this using the formula...

Acceleration from A to B = $\frac{0\text{m/s}}{5\text{s}}$ = **0m/s²**

B to C: Substitute figures into the formula...

Deceleration from B to C = $\frac{-15\text{m/s}}{4\text{s}}$ = **-3.75m/s²**

So, the object accelerated at 5m/s^2 for 3 seconds, travelled at a constant speed of 15m/s for 5 seconds before decelerating at a rate of -3.75m/s^2 for 4 seconds.

The total distance travelled can be calculated by working out the area under the velocity–time graph.

= Area of 0AX + Area of ABYX + Area of BCY

= $(\frac{1}{2} \times 3 \times 15) + (5 \times 15) + (\frac{1}{2} \times 4 \times 15)$ = **127.5m**

12.2

How do we make things speed up or slow down?

To change the speed of an object, an unbalanced force must act on it. To understand this, you need to know…

- what forces act on objects
- the factors that affect the motion of an object
- how force, mass and acceleration are related
- about stopping distances
- what terminal velocity is.

Forces

Forces are pushes or pulls. They are measured in **newtons (N)** and may vary in size and act in different directions.

When a stationary object rests on a surface it exerts a **downward force** (weight). The surface it rests on exerts an **upward force** (reaction). These two forces are equal and opposite and therefore the object remains stationary.

A number of forces acting on an object can be replaced by a single force which has the same effect on the object as the original forces all acting together. This is called the **resultant force**.

Friction

Friction is a force that occurs when an object moves through a medium, e.g. air or water, or when surfaces slide past each other. It works against the object, in the opposite direction to which it is moving.

When a motor vehicle travels at a steady speed, the frictional forces exactly balance the driving force.

Stopping Distance

The stopping distance of a vehicle depends on…

- **the thinking distance** – the distance travelled by the vehicle from the point when the driver realises he / she needs to stop to when he / she actually applies the brakes
- **the braking distance** – the distance travelled by the vehicle from the point when the driver applies the brakes to where the vehicle eventually stops.

Stopping distance = Thinking distance + Braking distance

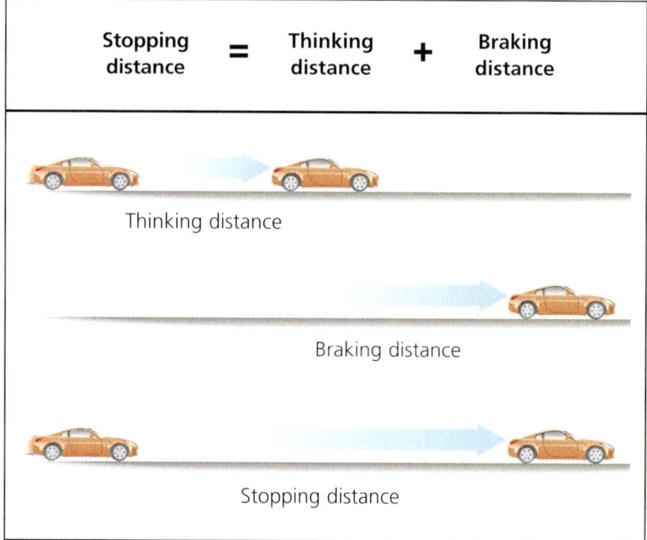

The overall stopping distance is increased if…

- the vehicle is travelling at greater speeds.
  - At 50mph the stopping distance is about 50m, equal to half the length of a football pitch.
  - At 70mph the stopping distance is about 100m, equal to the length of a football pitch.
- there are adverse weather conditions, e.g. wet or icy roads, poor visibility, etc.
  - On a dry road at 50mph the stopping distance is about 50m.
  - On a wet or greasy road at 50mph the stopping distance is about 80m.
- the driver is tired or under the influence of drugs or alcohol and cannot react as quickly as normal
- the vehicle is in a poor condition, e.g. underinflated tyres.

The greater the speed of the vehicle the greater the braking force needed to stop in a certain time.

How Forces Affect Movement

The movement of an object depends on the forces acting upon it.

If they are equal and opposite, the forces acting are balanced. If they are not equal and opposite, then they are unbalanced.

Object	Resultant Forces	
	Zero (Balanced)	Not Zero (Unbalanced)
Stationary	• Object remains stationary.	• Object will start to move in the direction of the resultant force.
Moving at a constant speed	• Object will continue at same constant speed in same direction.	• Object will speed up or slow down in the direction of the resultant force.

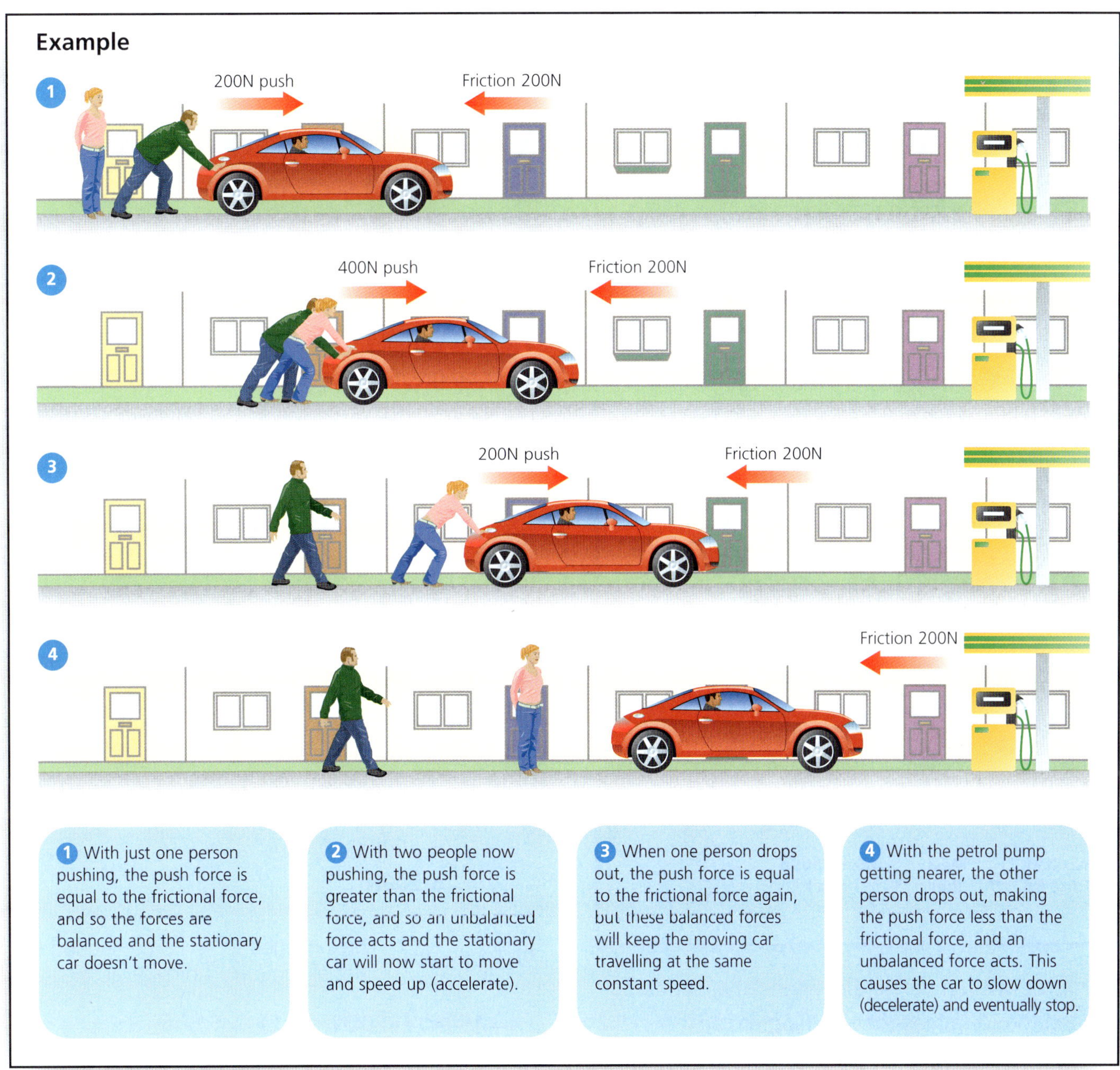

Force, Mass and Acceleration

If an unbalanced force acts on an object then the acceleration of the object will depend on...

- the **size** of the unbalanced force – the bigger the force, the greater the acceleration
- the **mass** of the object – the bigger the mass, the smaller the acceleration.

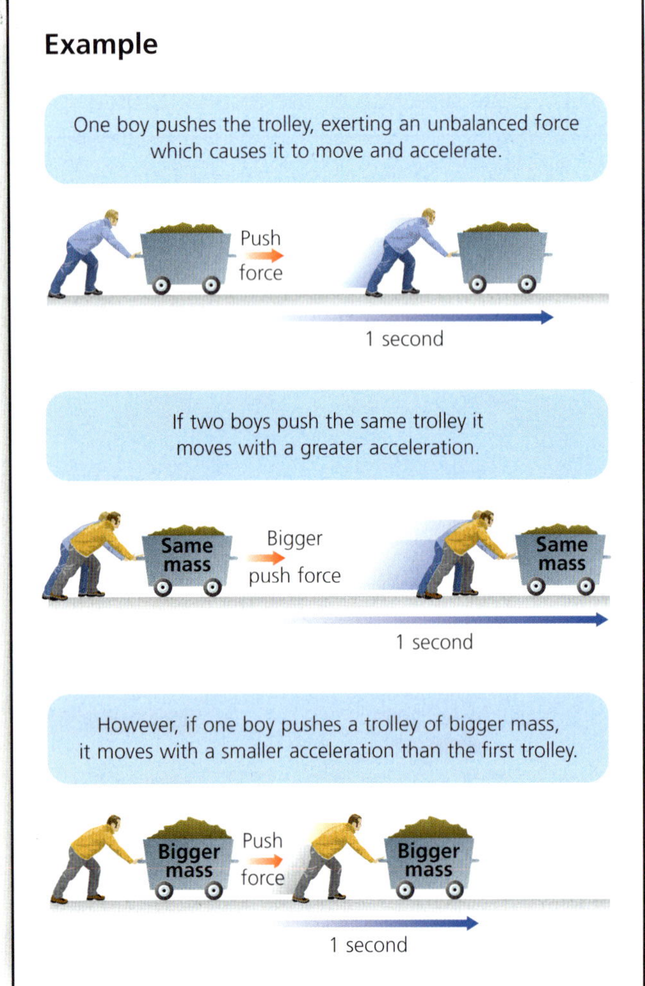

The relationship between force, mass and acceleration is shown in the following formula...

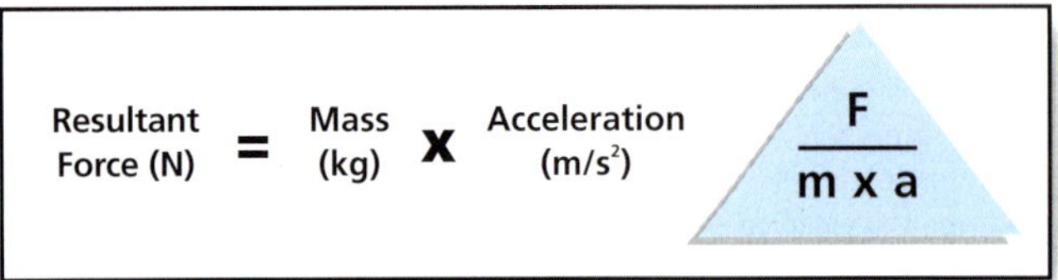

From this, we can define a newton (N) as the force needed to give a mass of one kilogram an acceleration of one metre per second squared ($1m/s^2$).

Example

A trolley of mass 400kg is pushed along a floor with a constant speed by one boy who exerts a push force of 150N.

Another boy joins him to increase the push force and the trolley accelerates at $0.5m/s^2$. Calculate...

a) the force needed to achieve this acceleration
b) the total push force exerted on the trolley.

Initially the trolley is moving at a constant speed, so the forces acting on it must be balanced.

Therefore, the 150N push force must be opposed by an equal force, i.e. friction or air resistance.

When the trolley starts accelerating the push force must be greater than friction, etc. These forces do not cancel each other out and an unbalanced force now acts.

a) Using the formula:

Force = Mass x Acceleration
= $400kg \times 0.5m/s^2$
= 200N

b) Total push = Force needed to equal friction + Force needed to provide acceleration

= 150N + 200N
= 350N

Terminal Velocity

Falling objects experience two forces...

- the downward force of weight, W (↓) which always stays the same
- the upward force of air resistance, R, or drag (↑).

When a skydiver jumps out of an aeroplane, the speed of his descent can be considered in two separate part – before and after the paracute opens:

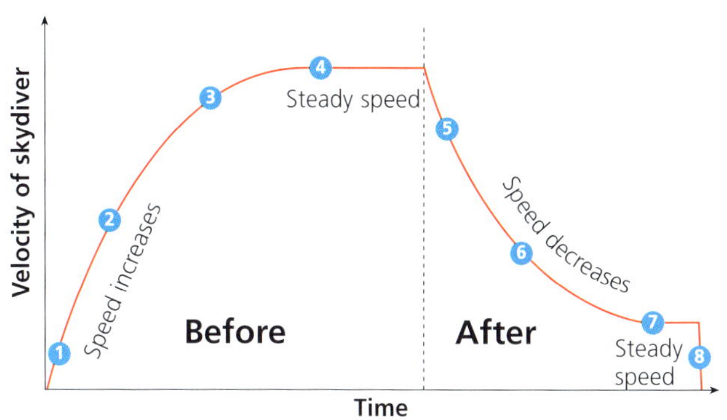

Before the Parachute Opens

When the skydiver jumps, he initially accelerates due to the force of gravity (see ❶). Gravity is a force of attraction that acts between objects that have mass, e.g. the skydiver and the Earth. The weight of an object is the force exerted on it by gravity. It is measured in newtons (N).

However, as the skydiver falls he experiences the frictional force of air resistance (R) in the opposite direction. But this is not as great as W so he continues to accelerate (see ❷).

As his speed increases, so does the air resistance acting on him (see ❸), until eventually R is equal to W (see ❹). This means that the resultant force acting on him is now zero and his falling speed becomes constant. This speed is called the **terminal velocity**.

After the Parachute Opens

When the parachute is opened, unbalanced forces act again because the upward force of R is now greatly increased and is bigger than W (see ❺). This decreases his speed and as his speed decreases so does R (see ❻).

Eventually R decreases until it is equal to W (see ❼). The forces acting are once again balanced and for the second time he falls at a steady speed, slower than before though, i.e. at a new terminal velocity.

How Science Works

You need to be able to draw and interpret velocity–time graphs for bodies that reach terminal velocity, including a consideration of the forces acting on the body.

Example

A peregrin falcon is flying above the ground at a velocity of 25m/s. After 10 seconds, it spots a mouse on the ground and goes into a vertical dive making itself into a streamlined shape. It takes 15 seconds for the bird to reach a terminal velocity of 95m/s. It then sustains terminal velocity for 5 seconds. This information can be plotted on a velocity–time graph…

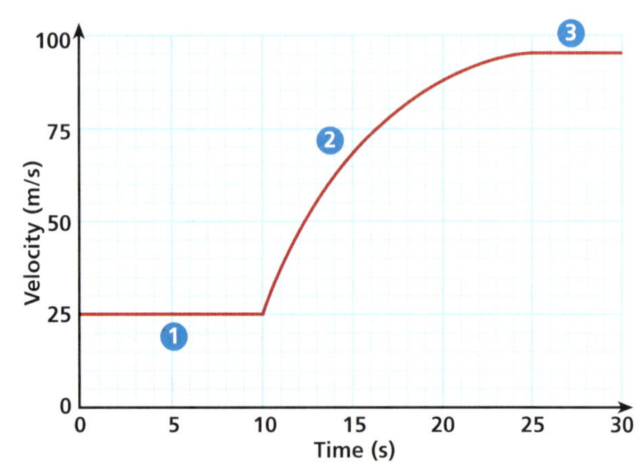

1. The flat line at the start of the graph shows the bird flying at a constant velocity.

2. The curve of the graph begins when the bird enters the dive. The line is steep at first showing fast acceleration. The line gradually becomes less steep because the air resistance acting against the bird slows down acceleration.

3. The flat line at the top of the graph shows the bird has reached terminal velocity and is travelling through the air at a constant velocity.

You need to be able to calculate the weight of a body using the following formula…

Weight (Newton, N)	=	Mass (Kilogram, kg)	x	Gravitational field strength (Newton/kilogram, N/kg)

Gravitational field strength is the force that acts on a 1kg mass at a point in a gravitational field. It is measured in newtons per kilogram (N/kg).

Example

The Earth's surface has a gravitational field strength of approximately 10N/kg. The Moon has a gravitational field strength approximately $\frac{1}{6}$ of the Earth's. That means that an object weighs less on the Moon that it does on Earth.

If an astronaut has a mass of 85kg…

- his weight on Earth = 85kg x 10N/kg = **850N**
- his weight on Moon = 85kg x $\frac{10}{6}$ N/kg = **141.7N**

12.3

What happens to the movement energy when things speed up or slow down?

When an object speeds up or slows down, its kinetic (movement) energy increases or decreases by transferring energy to or from the object. To understand this, you need to know...

- that work done equals energy transferred
- how work done, force and distance are related
- how mass and speed determine kinetic energy
- the result of friction against work done
- how to calculate kinetic energy.

Work

When a force moves an object, work is done on the object resulting in the transfer of energy. Energy is measured in **joules (J)**. Therefore...

Work done (J) = Energy transferred (J)

The relationship between work done, force and distance is shown by the following formula...

Work done (J) = Force applied (N) X Distance moved in direction of force (m)

$$\frac{J}{N \times m}$$

Example

A man pushes a car with a steady force of 250N. The car moves a distance of 20m. How much work does the man do?

Work done = Force applied x Distance moved
= 250N x 20m
= **5000J (or 5kJ)**

Work done against frictional forces is mainly transformed into heat energy. For an object that is able to recover its original shape, elastic potential is the energy stored in the object when work is done on the object to change its shape.

Kinetic Energy

Kinetic energy is the energy an object has because of its movement. It depends on two things: the **mass** of the object (kg) and the **speed** of the object (m/s).

Example

A moving car has kinetic energy as it has both mass and speed. As it moves with a greater speed, its mass is unchanged but it has more kinetic energy.

However, a moving truck has a greater mass than the car, so even if it is going slower than the car, it may have more kinetic energy.

Kinetic energy is calculated by this formula...

Kinetic energy (J) = $\frac{1}{2}$ X Mass (kg) X Speed^2 (m/s)^2

$$\frac{K.E.}{\frac{1}{2} \times m \times v^2}$$

Example

A car of mass 1000kg is moving at a speed of 10m/s. How much kinetic energy does it have?

Using the formula...

Kinetic energy = $\frac{1}{2}$ x Mass x Speed^2
= $\frac{1}{2}$ x 1000kg x (10m/s)^2
= **50 000J (or 50kJ)**

How Science Works

You need to be able to discuss the transformation of kinetic energy to other forms of energy in particular situations.

Example 1: Space Shuttles

When a space shuttle returns to Earth it has a lot of kinetic energy, i.e. it has a large mass and is travelling fast. As it enters the Earth's atmosphere, the shuttle encounters frictional forces and the kinetic energy is transformed into heat energy which slows it down.

The shuttle can reach extremely high temperatures because of the heat energy produced, which causes a risk of fire and explosion. Scientists have developed special heat shields to try to protect the body of space shuttles (and the astronauts in them) from this intense heat.

Example 2: Hydroelectricity

Hydroelectric power stations use the kinetic energy in moving water to produce electricity. A dam is built across a river valley and water builds up behind it. The water held behind the dam contains potential energy.

This potential energy is transformed to kinetic energy when the water is released down tubes inside the dam. The moving water is used to drive generators which transform the kinetic energy into electrical energy.

Example 3: Bungee Rides

A bungee ride consists of a spherical cage that is attached to two supporting arms by elastic cords. Just before the ride starts, the bungee cords are tightened which provides the elastic potential energy.

When the cage (attached to the cord) is released, the elastic potential energy contained in the cord is transformed into kinetic energy which propels the cage straight up into the air. The kinetic energy of the cage is reduced as it travels upwards (against the force of gravity, and due to air resistance) and the cord becomes stretched, so the remaining kinetic energy is transformed into elastic potential energy.

When the cord reaches the limit of its elasticity (at the top) the elastic potential energy is again transformed back into kinetic energy and the cage travels down towards the Earth again, assisted by gravity, but again, the force is reduced by air resistance. The kinetic energy is transformed back into elastic energy as the cord is stretched, until it reaches its limit of elasticity (which is less than the limit reached initially due to the energy that has been lost).

The elastic energy is transformed back into kinetic energy, the cage starts to move upwards again and the process is repeated with decreasing amounts of energy each time, until it is stopped.

12.4

What is momentum?

A moving object has momentum as well as kinetic energy. When looking at what happens to objects as a result of an explosion or collision, it is more useful to think in terms of momentum. To understand this, you need to know...

- how momentum, mass and velocity are related
- that momentum has both magnitude and direction
- what factors affect momentum
- how force, change in momentum and time taken for change are related (Higher Tier).

What is Momentum?

Momentum is a measure of the state of motion of an object. It is dependent upon two things:

- the mass of the object (kg)
- the velocity of the object (m/s) (see p.40).

A moving car has momentum as it has both mass and velocity. If the car moves with a greater velocity, it has more momentum providing its mass has not changed. However, a moving truck with a greater mass may have more momentum than the car even if its velocity is less.

The momentum of an object is calculated using the following formula:

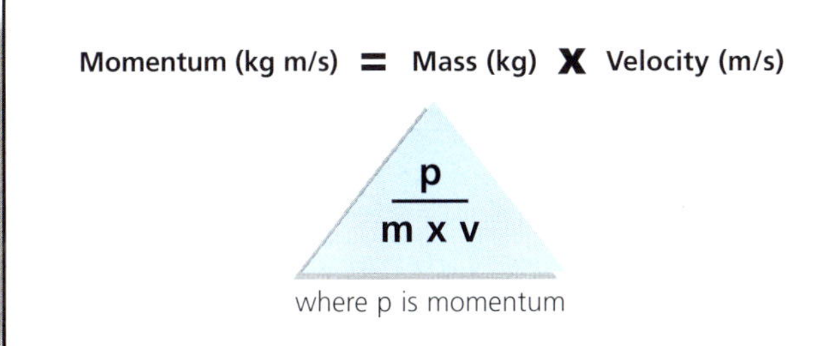

Example 1

A car has a mass of 1200kg. It is travelling at a velocity of 30m/s. Calculate its momentum.

Using the formula...

Momentum = Mass x Velocity

= 1200kg x 30m/s = **36 000kg m/s**

Example 2

A truck has a mass of 4000kg. Calculate its velocity if it has the same momentum as the car in Example 1.

Using the formula (rearranged using the formula triangle)...

$$\textbf{Velocity} = \frac{\textbf{Momentum}}{\textbf{Mass}} = \frac{36\,000\text{kg m/s}}{4000\text{kg}} = \textbf{9m/s}$$

p
m x

Since the truck has a greater mass than the car it can move at a slower speed and still have the same momentum.

Magnitude and Direction

Velocity and momentum are both quantities which have magnitude (size) and direction. The direction of movement is especially important when calculating momentum. For example...

If Car A (which is moving from left to right) has a positive velocity and, consequently, a positive momentum, then Car B (moving from right to left) will have a negative velocity and negative momentum because it is moving in the opposite direction to Car A.

Example

If car A has a mass of 1000kg and a velocity of 20m/s, then...

momentum = 1000kg x 20m/s

= **20 000kg m/s**

If car B has a mass of 1000kg and a velocity of -20m/s...

momentum = 1000kg x -20m/s

= **-20 000kg m/s**

Force and Change in Momentum

When a force acts on a moving object, or a stationary object that is capable of moving, the object will experience a change in momentum.

An external force can...

- give a stationary object momentum (i.e. make it move)
- increase the momentum of a moving object
- decrease, or completely take away (i.e. stop), the momentum of a moving object.

The extent of the change in momentum depends on the size of the force and the length of time it is acting on the object.

Force, change in momentum and the time taken for the change are related by the following formula...

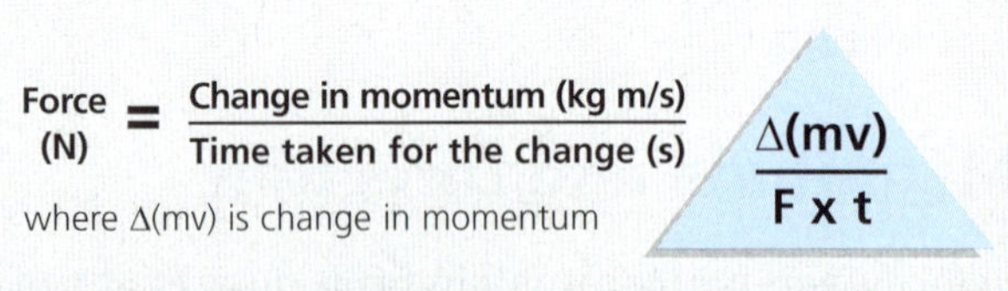

Example

A girl kicks a stationary ball with a force of 30N. The force acts on the ball for 0.15 seconds. If the mass of the ball is 0.5kg, calculate...

a) the change in momentum of the ball and

b) the increase in velocity of the ball.

a) Rearranging the formula...

Change in momentum = Force x Time
= 30N x 0.15s
= **4.5kg m/s**

b) We can now work out the increase in velocity of the ball using the formula from page 51.

$$\text{Velocity} = \frac{\text{Momentum}}{\text{Mass}} = \frac{4.5\text{kg m/s}}{0.5\text{kg}} = \mathbf{9m/s}$$

The girl can increase the change in momentum of the ball, and as a result its velocity, without increasing the force applied by 'following through' with her kick. Doing this will increase the time for which the force is applied. Some sports where following through increases the velocity of the ball are cricket, golf, tennis and squash.

Collisions and Explosions

In any collision or explosion, the momentum in a particular direction after the event is the same as the momentum in that direction before the event, i.e. Momentum is **conserved,** provided that **no** external forces act.

Example 1

Two cars are travelling in the same direction along a road. Car A collides with the back of Car B and they stick together. Calculate their velocity after the collision.

Before

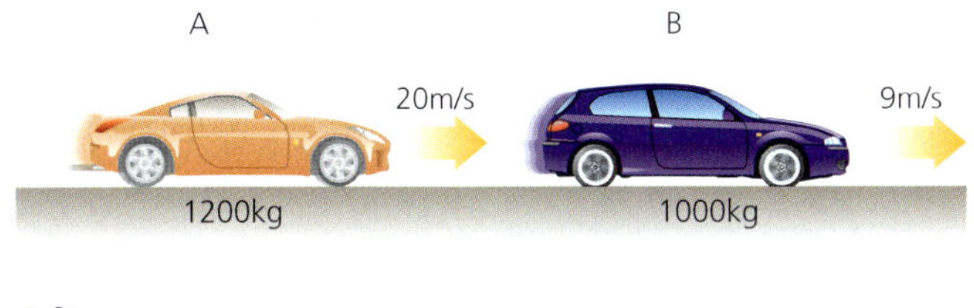

After

Momentum before collision...

= Momentum of A + Momentum of B
= (Mass x velocity of A) + (Mass x velocity of B)
= (1200kg x 20m/s) + (1000kg x 9m/s)
= 24 000kg m/s + 9000kg m/s
= 33 000kg m/s

Momentum after collision...

= Momentum of A and B stuck together
= (1200+1000) x v
= 2200v

Since momentum is conserved...

Total momentum before = Total momentum after

$$33\,000 = 2200v$$

$$\text{Therefore, } v = \frac{33\,000}{2200} = \mathbf{15m/s}$$

Example 2

A gun fires a bullet of mass 0.01kg as shown below. The velocity of the bullet is 350m/s. Calculate the recoil velocity of the gun.

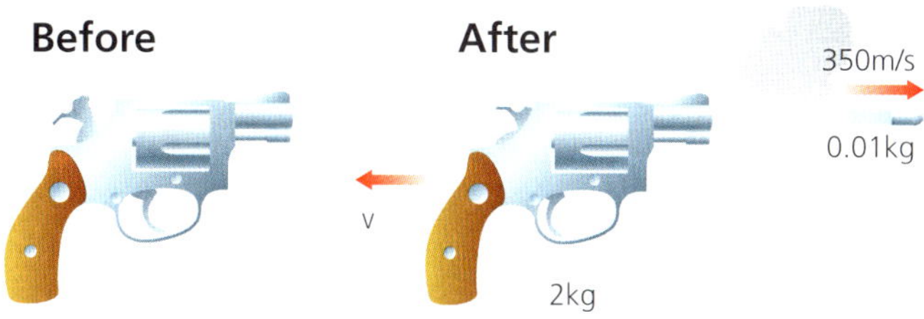

Firing a gun is an example of an explosion where the two objects, i.e. the gun and the bullet, move away from each other, rather than come towards each other as in a collision.

As we have seen, velocity and momentum are quantities that have magnitude and direction.

Since the gun and the bullet are moving in opposite directions, we will assume that the bullet has positive velocity and momentum which means that the gun has negative velocity and momentum.

Momentum before explosion = 0
(Neither the gun nor the bullet have momentum as they are not moving.)

Momentum after explosion...

= Momentum of bullet + Momentum of gun
= (Mass x velocity of bullet) + (Mass x velocity of gun)
= (0.01kg x 350m/s) + (2kg x -v)
= 3.5 – 2v

Since momentum is conserved...

Momentum after explosion = Momentum before explosion
Momentum of bullet and momentum of gun = 0
(mass x velocity of bullet) + (mass x velocity of gun) = 0
(0.01kg x 350m/s) + (2kg x v) = 0

$$3.5 + 2v = 0$$
$$2v = -3.5$$
$$v = \frac{-3.5}{2}$$
$$v = \mathbf{-1.75m/s}$$

Remember, the gun is moving in the opposite direction to the bullet so it has negative velocity.

How Science Works

You need to be able to use the ideas of momentum to explain safety features.

We already know that momentum is conserved in a collision (see p.53). This means that if a vehicle is brought to a sudden halt or makes a sudden change in direction, the people in the vehicle will continue with the same momentum as before. In other words, any people in the vehicle will continue to travel at the same speed and in the same direction as they were travelling immediately *before* the change.

Obviously, this can have fatal consequences, so cars have inbuilt safety features to try to minimise injury and reduce the number of deaths.

Example 1: Seat Belts

Seat belts lock when a car crashes. They exert a force to counteract the momentum of the person wearing them. This prevents the wearer from flying through the windscreen or smashing against the inside of the car.

Cars travelling at faster speeds have greater momentum. This means that at high speeds the seatbelt has to exert a larger opposing force which can result in some bruising and injuries. However, the injuries caused by a seatbelt will be a lot less severe than those it prevents.

Example 2: Crumple Zones

A crumple zone is an area designed to 'crumple' on impact. This helps to increase the time over which the car changes momentum, i.e. instead of coming to an immediate halt there will be a few seconds during which the momentum is reduced. This means that the force exerted on the people inside the car will be reduced, which results in fewer injuries.

Example 3: Power-assisted steering and anti-lock braking systems (ABS)

These help the driver to control direction and speed, which can help to reduce change in momentum.

Example 4: Air bags

Air bags only partially inflate on impact so they are 'squashy'. They distribute the force of impact more evenly over the upper body area and reduce the momentum of the body more gradually.

12.5

What is static electricity, how can it be used and what is the connection between static electricity and electric currents?

Static electricity can be explained in terms of electrical charges; when electrical charges move they create an electric current.
To understand this, you need to know...

- how materials become electrically charged
- about repulsion and attraction
- how conductors are used
- how electrostatic charges are used.

Static Electricity

Some insulating materials can become electrically charged when they are rubbed against each other. The electrical charge (static) then stays on the material (i.e. it is not discharged).

You can generate static electricity by rubbing a balloon against a jumper. The electrically charged balloon will then attract very small objects.

Static builds up when electrons (which have a negative charge) are 'rubbed off' one material onto another. The material receiving the electrons becomes negatively charged and the one giving up electrons becomes positively charged.

For example, if you rub a Perspex rod with a cloth, the Perspex loses electrons to become positively charged. The cloth gains electrons to become negatively charged.

If you rub an ebonite rod with a fur, ebonite gains electrons to become negatively charged. Fur loses electrons to become positively charged.

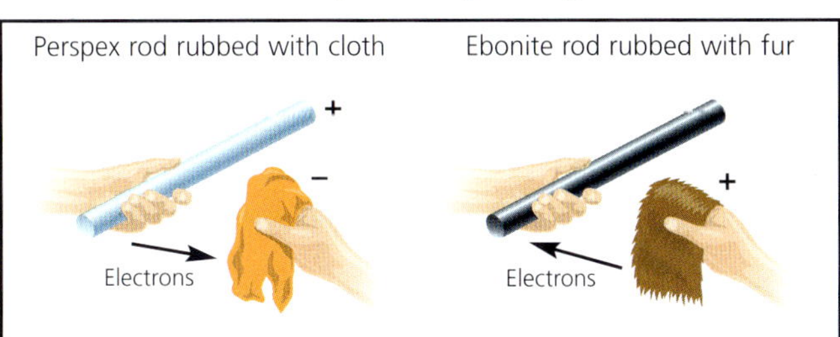

Repulsion and Attraction

When two charged materials are brought together, they exert a force on each other so they are attracted or repelled. Two materials with the same type of charge repel each other; two materials with different types of charge attract each other.

If you move a Perspex rod near to a suspended Perspex rod, the suspended Perspex rod will be repelled.

If you move an ebonite rod near to a suspended Perspex rod, the suspended Perspex rod will be attracted.

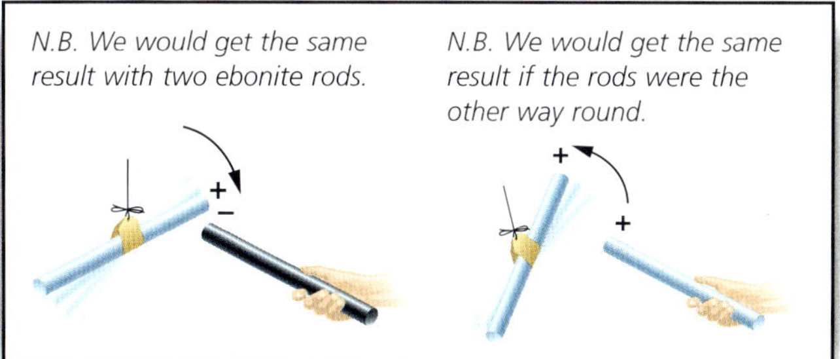

The Uses of Static

Electrostatic charges can be very useful in industry and at home. They can be used in a variety of different ways, for example...

- reducing air pollution
- air fresheners
- photocopiers
- painting cars in the automobile industry.

Electrostatic Smoke Precipitator

Smoke precipitators are designed to remove solid smoke particles from waste gases before the gases are released into the environment.

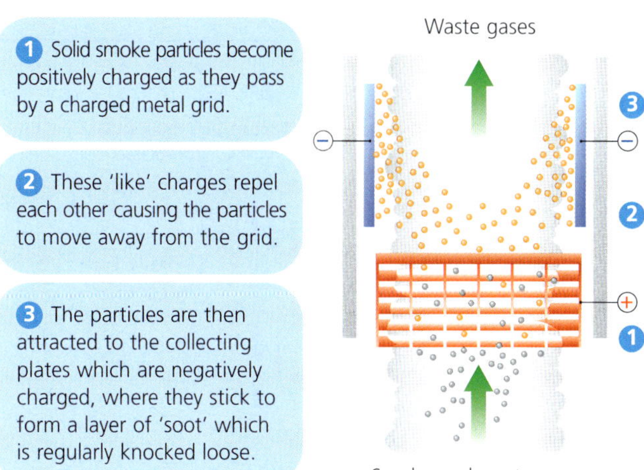

The Uses of Static (cont.)

The Photocopier

An image of the page to be copied is projected onto an electrically charged plate (usually positively charged).

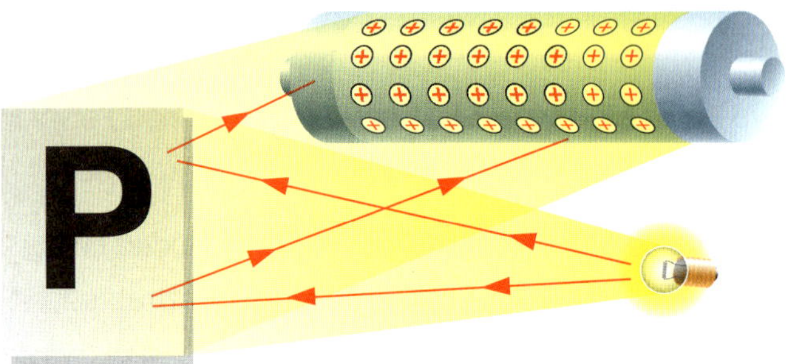

Light causes charge to leak away, leaving an electrostatic impression of the page.

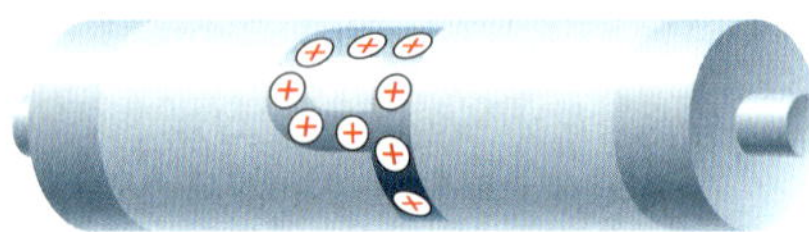

This charged impression on the plate attracts tiny specks of black powder, which is then transferred from the plate to paper. Heat is used to fix the final image on the paper.

Discharge of Static Electricity

A charged conductor (positive or negative) can be discharged, i.e. have any charge on it removed, by connecting it to earth with a conductor.

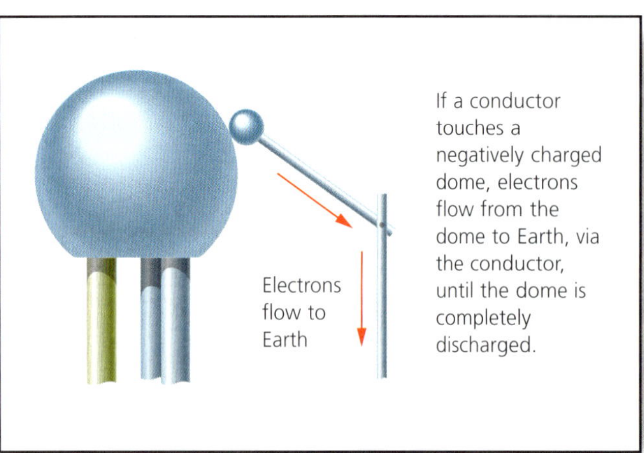

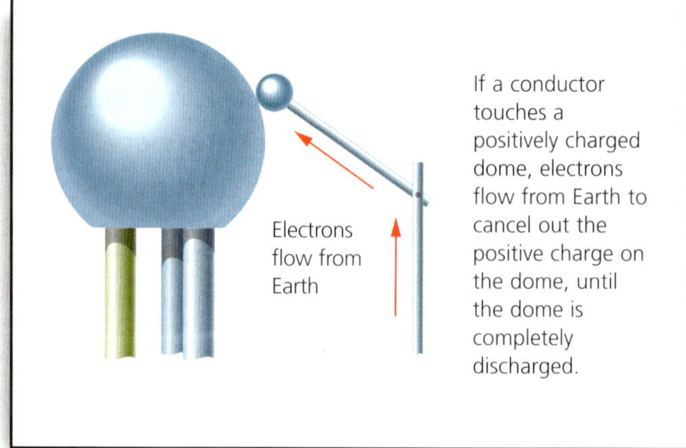

This flow of electrons through a solid conductor is an electric current. Metals conduct electricity well because electrons from their atoms can move freely throughout the metal structure.

HT The greater the charge on an isolated object, the greater the potential difference between the object and Earth.

If the potential difference between the object and a nearby earthed conductor becomes high enough, a spark may jump across the gap between the object and conductor.

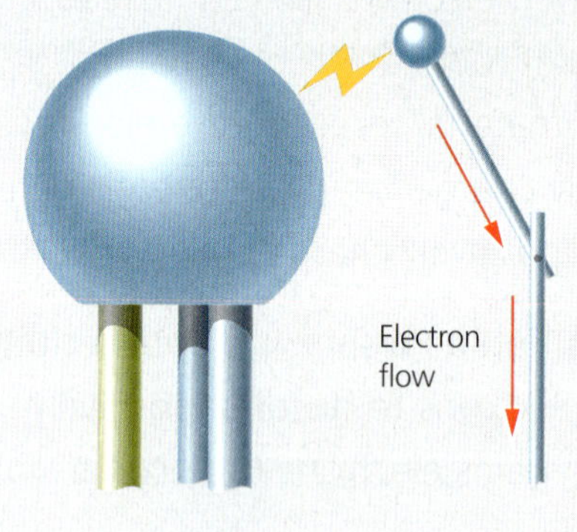

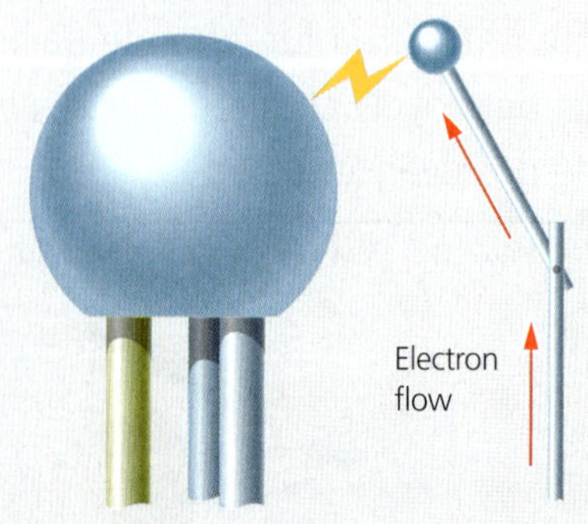

You need to be able to explain why static electricity is dangerous in some situations and how precautions can be taken to ensure that the electrostatic charge is discharged safely.

Static electricity can create a spark or make people experience a mild electric shock when certain objects are touched. This is because certain materials, including dry human skin, can build up charges which then create a spark when something else is touched.

Although they can be slightly painful, these types of electric shocks are not dangerous or destructive. In some situations, however, static can be very hazardous and precautions need to be taken to ensure that it is safely discharged.

Example 1: Petrol Stations

When petrol is transferred either from a truck to the petrol station, or from the petrol pumps into our cars, a lot of friction is created. If a static charge is discharged in such an area, the results can be disastrous – a single spark could ignite the petrol vapours and cause an explosion. Therefore, when trucks transfer petrol into the petrol station, they use a grounding device on the hose that draws the electrical charges away from the petrol. This prevents any static sparks from occurring.

When filling a car with petrol you should...

- turn the engine off
- touch something metal when you get out of your car to get rid of any excess charges, e.g. from car seat materials
- avoid using mobile phones
- place petrol containers on the ground when filling them up

Example 2: Refuelling Planes

During refuelling, the fuel gains electrons from the fuel pipe, making the pipe positively charged and the fuel negatively charged. The resulting voltage between the two can cause a spark (discharge) which could cause a major explosion. To prevent this, either of the following can be done:

- earth the fuel tank with a copper conductor
- link the tanker and the plane with a copper conductor.

Example 3: Working on Computers

The internal electronics of a computer can be easily damaged by an electrical spark. To reduce the chance of this happening, technicians working on the inside of computers use a special pad on the floor and a grounded strap on their wrist. This takes any static charges away from their bodies before any damage can be done.

You need to be able to explain why static electricity is dangerous in some situations and how precautions can be taken to ensure that the electrostatic charge is discharged safely. (Continued from previous page).

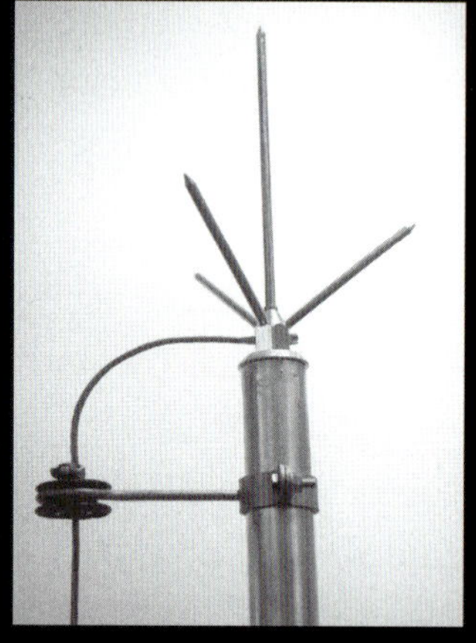

Lightning and Buildings

During a thunderstorm, lightning bolts are attracted to the highest point in the area. Therefore, buildings can often be hit and damaged. To control the force of the electricity, lightning rods are attached to the top of a building (a rod is a piece of metal which runs from the very top of the building down to the ground). If lightning does then strike, it would hit the metal lightning rod (the highest part of the structure) and the current would flow down through the rod into the ground, where it would be safely discharged, with minimal damage to the building.

Lightning and People

Getting hit by lightning is rare but it can happen, and normally causes serious injury or death. However, there are some things you can do to reduce the chances of being hit:

- avoid holding anything metal as this can attract lightning – playing golf during a thunderstorm is not advised
- try to be inside something that is grounded, e.g. a house or car. The inside of a car is normally fairly safe, as the rubber tyres will help to ground the electricity in the event of being hit.
- avoid standing under a tree during a storm – it might be the highest point in the area.

12.6

What does the current through an electrical circuit depend on?

The size of the push and the resistance determine the size of the current of the circuit. A supply tries to push a charge through a circuit and the circuit resists the charge. To understand this, you need to know...

- what affects the current in a circuit
- how potential difference, current and resistance are related
- which factors affect resistance
- what current–potential difference graphs show
- the differences between components connected in series and in parallel.

Circuits

An electric current will flow through an electrical component (or device) if there is a voltage or potential difference (p.d.) across the ends of the component.

In the following circuits, each cell and lamp are identical.

Circuit 1

Cell provides p.d. across the lamp. A current flows and the lamp lights up.

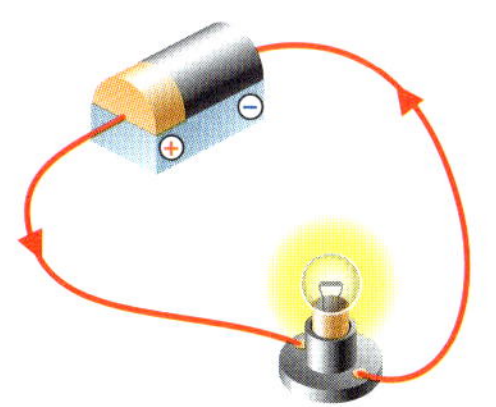

The amount of current that flows through the component depends on...

- the potential difference across the component
- the resistance of the component.

The Potential Difference Across the Component

The greater the potential difference (voltage) across a component, the greater the current that flows through the component.

Circuit 2

Two cells together provide a bigger p.d. across the lamp. A bigger current now flows and the lamp lights up more brightly (compared to circuit 1).

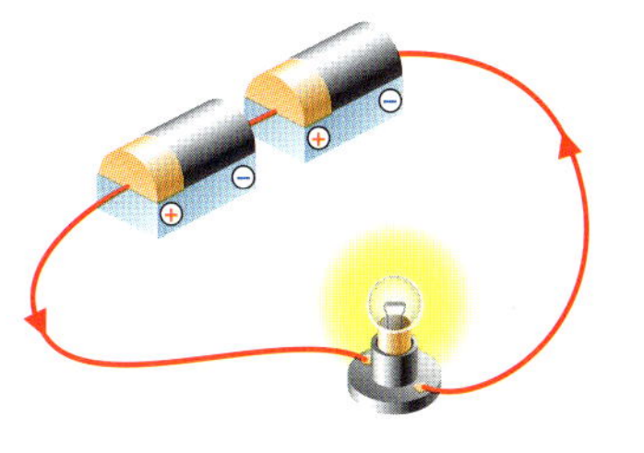

The Resistance of the Component

Components resist the flow of current through them, i.e. they have **resistance** (measured in ohms). The greater the resistance of a component or components, the smaller the current that flows for a particular voltage, or the greater the voltage needed to maintain a particular current.

Circuit 3

Two lamps together have a greater resistance. A smaller current now flows and the lamps light up less brightly (compared to circuit 1).

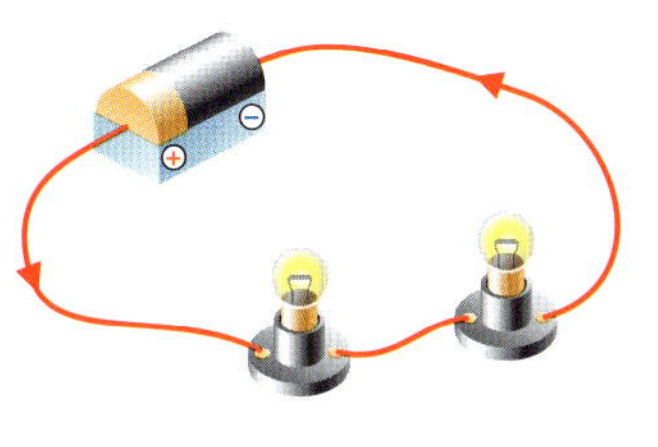

Circuit 4

Two cells together provide a greater voltage. The same current as in circuit 1 will now flow. The lamps light up more brightly than in circuit 3 (the same as circuit 1).

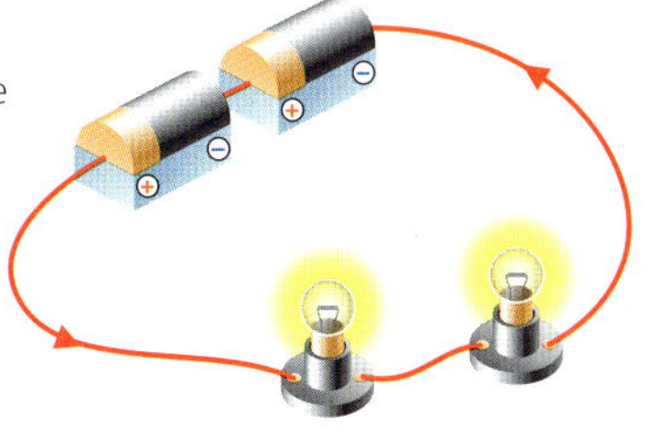

Potential Difference and Current

The potential difference across a component in a circuit is measured in **volts (V)** using a **voltmeter** connected in **parallel** across the component.

The current flowing through a component in a circuit is measured in **amperes (A),** using an **ammeter** connected in **series.**

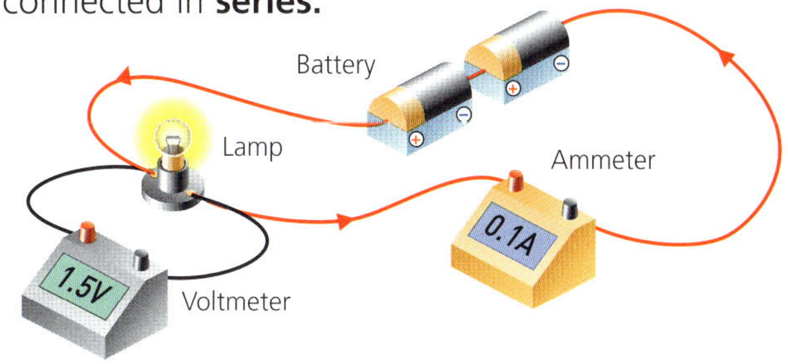

Unit 2

Resistance

Resistance is a measure of how hard it is to get a current through a component at a particular potential difference (voltage). Potential difference, current and resistance are related by the following formula:

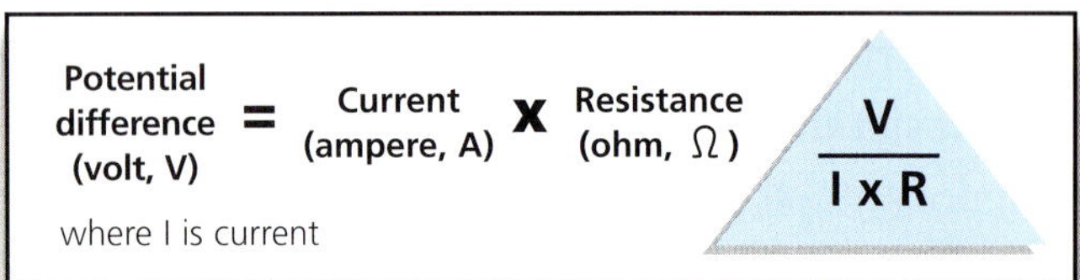

Example

Calculate the reading on the voltmeter in this circuit if the bulb has a resistance of 15 ohms.

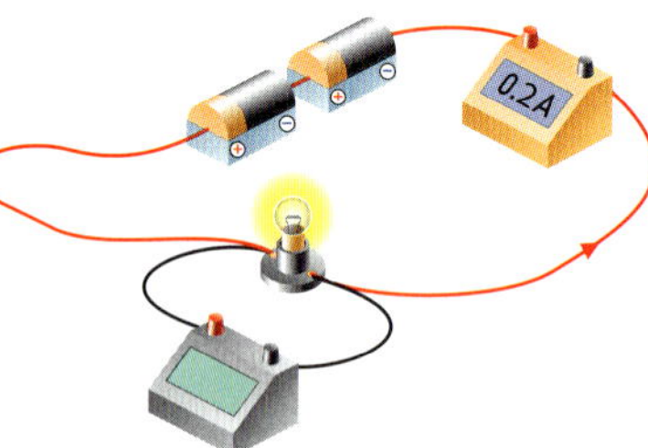

Use the formula...

Potential difference = Current x Resistance

= 0.2A x 15 Ω

= **3V**

The reading on the ammeter is the current.

Resistance of Components

These can be investigated using the circuit above with a power pack instead of batteries. You can then draw **current–potential difference graphs** which show how the current through the component varies with the voltage across it.

Resistors

As long as the temperature of the resistor stays constant, the current through the resistor is directly proportional to the voltage across the resistor, regardless of which direction the current is flowing, i.e. if one doubles, the other also doubles.

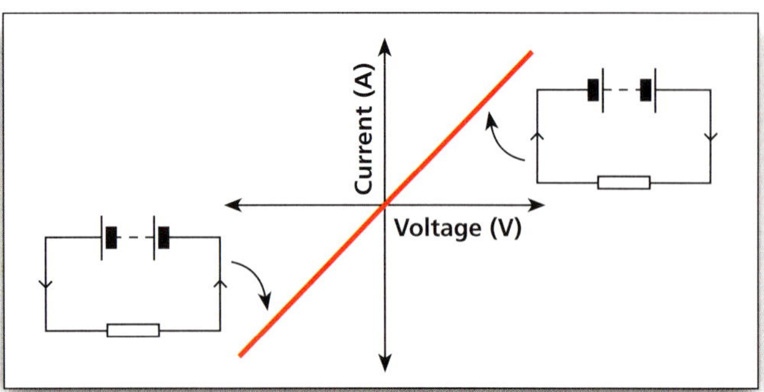

Filament Lamps

As the temperature of the filament increases and the bulb gets brighter then the resistance of the lamp increases, regardless of which direction the current is flowing.

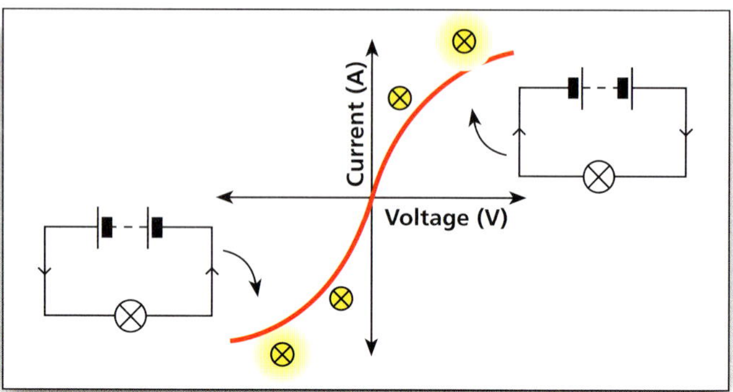

Diodes

A diode allows a current to flow through it in one direction only. It has a very high resistance in the reverse direction so no current flows.

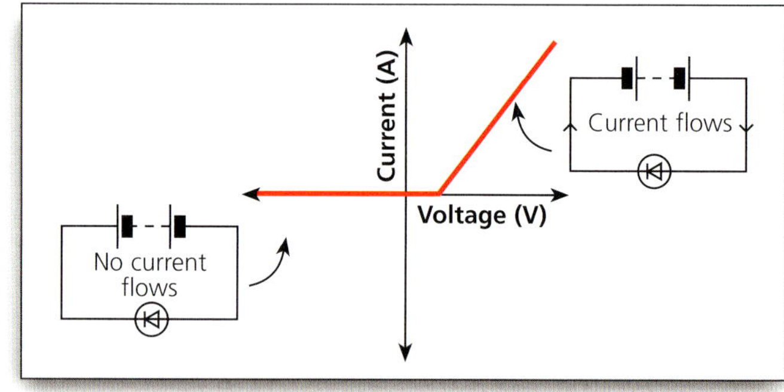

Light Dependent Resistor (LDR)

The resistance of an LDR depends on the amount of light falling on it. Its resistance decreases as the amount of light falling on it increases; this allows more current to flow.

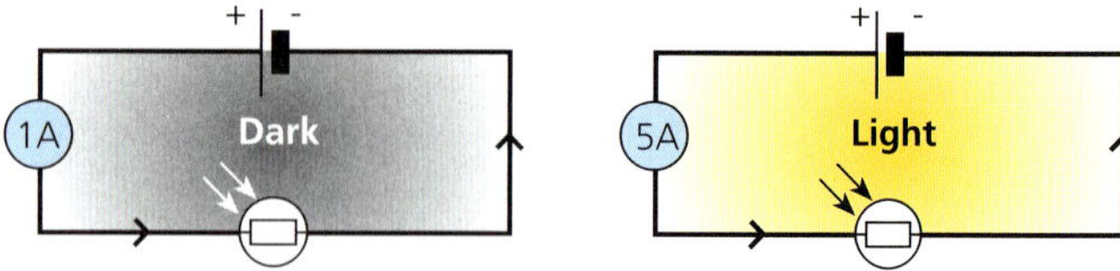

Thermistor

The resistance of a thermistor depends on its temperature. Its resistance decreases as the temperature of the thermistor increases; this allows more current to flow.

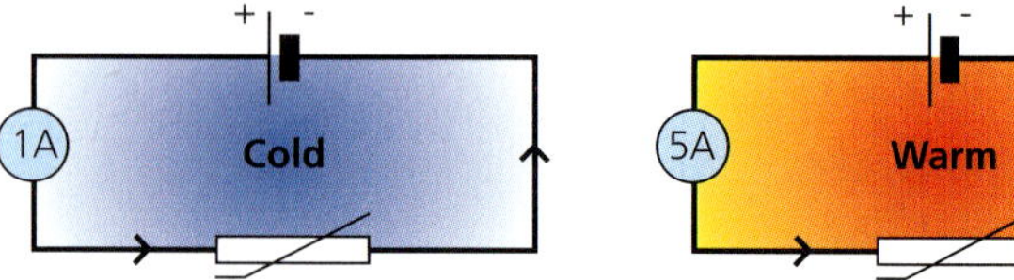

Series and Parallel Circuits

Components Connected in Series	Components Connected in Parallel
In a series circuit, all components are connected one after the other in one loop, going from one terminal of the battery to the other. 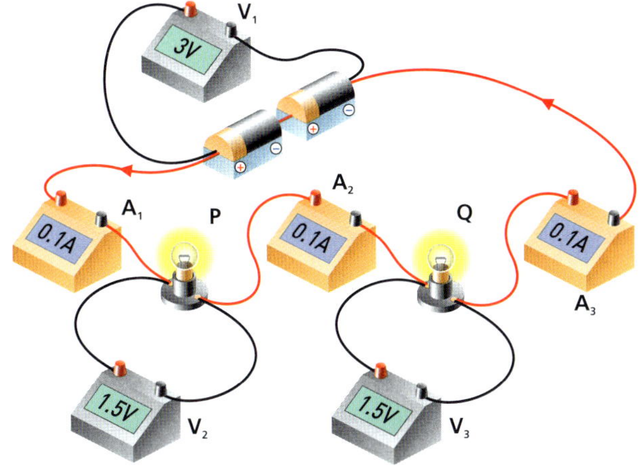 • The same current flows through each component, i.e. $\mathbf{A_1 = A_2 = A_3}$. In the circuit above, each ammeter reading is 0.1A. • The potential difference (voltage) supplied by the battery is divided up between the components in the circuit, i.e. $\mathbf{V_1 = V_2 + V_3}$. In the circuit above both bulbs have the same resistance so the potential difference is divided equally. If one bulb had twice the resistance of the other, then the potential difference would be divided differently, e.g. 2V and 1V. • The total resistance is the sum of the individual resistances of the components, i.e. $\Omega = \Omega_p + \Omega_Q$. In the circuit above, if both P and Q each have a resistance of 15 ohms, the total resistance would be 15 ohms + 15 ohms = 30 ohms.	Components connected in parallel are connected separately in their own loop going from one terminal of the battery to the other. 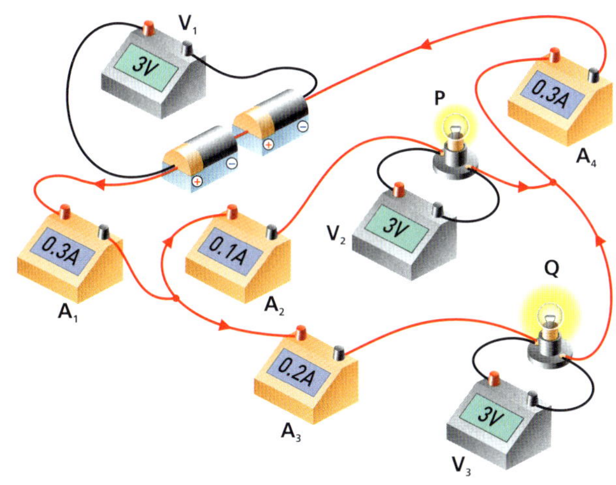 • The total current in the main circuit is equal to the sum of the currents through the separate components, i.e. $\mathbf{A_1 = A_2 + A_3 = A_4}$. In the circuit above, 0.3A = 0.1A + 0.2A = 0.3A. • The potential difference across each component is the same (and is equal to the p.d. of the battery) i.e. $\mathbf{V_1 = V_2 = V_3}$. In the circuit above, each bulb has a p.d. of 3V across it. • The amount of current which passes through a component depends on the resistance of the component. The greater the resistance, the smaller the current. In the circuit above, bulb P must have twice the resistance of bulb Q as only 0.1A passes through bulb P while 0.2A passes through bulb Q.

Connecting Cells in Series

The total potential difference provided by cells connected in series is the sum of the p.d. of each cell separately, providing that they have been connected in the same direction.

Each cell has a p.d. of 1.5V.

Total p.d. of battery
= 2 x 1.5V
= **3V**

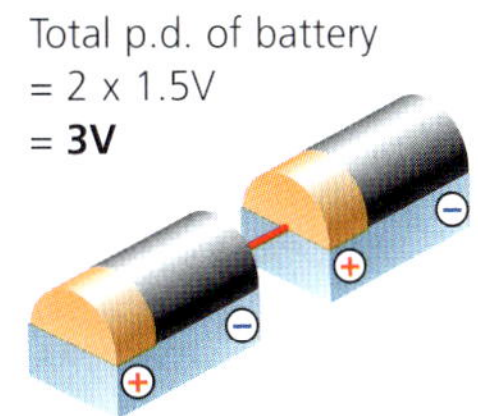

Total p.d. of battery
= 3 x 1.5V
= **4.5V**

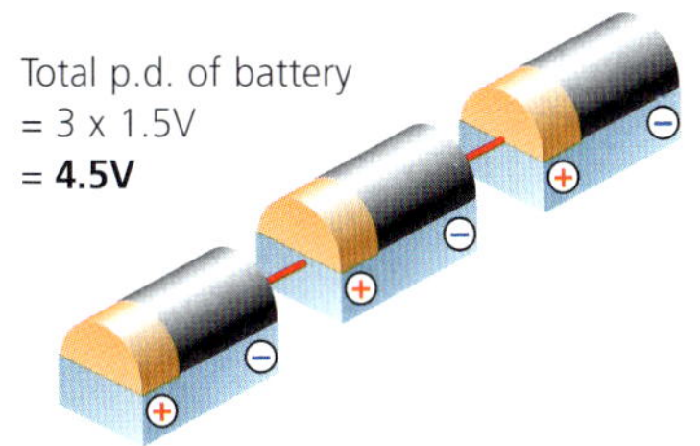

How Science Works

You should know the following standard symbols:

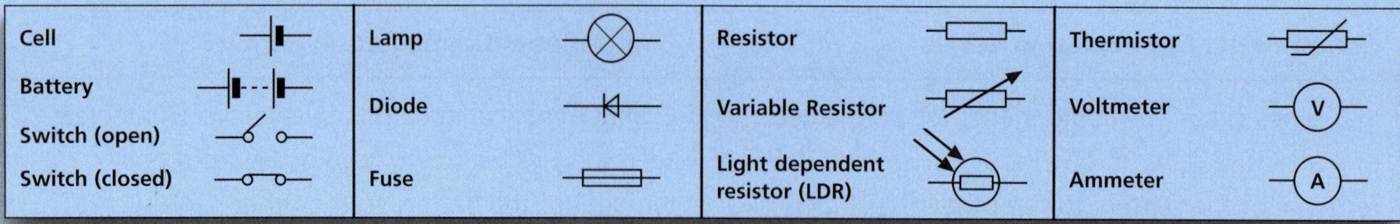

You need to be able to interpret and draw circuit diagrams using standard symbols.

Example 1

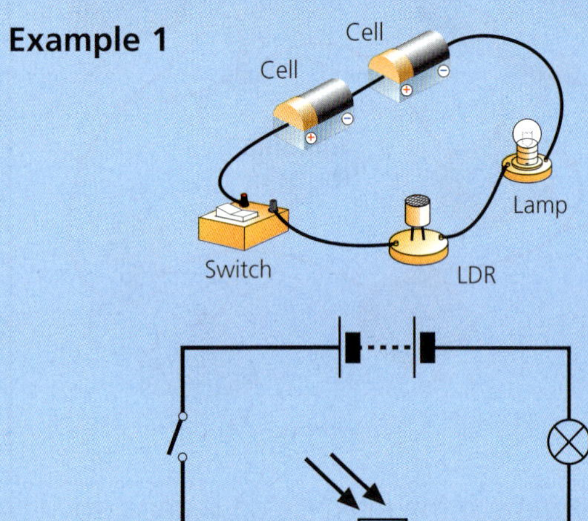

This is a series circuit. The light-dependent resistor is a variable resistor. When it is dark, it allows current through, but when more light falls on the sensor, its resistance increases and so less current is allowed through, making the light dimmer. This only happens when the switch is closed (which completes the circuit).

Example 2

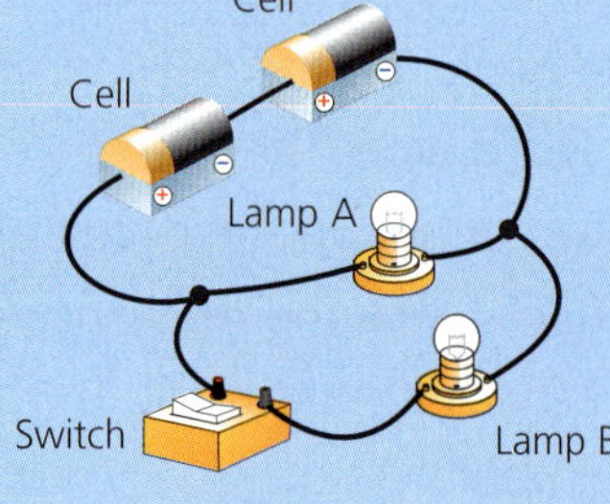

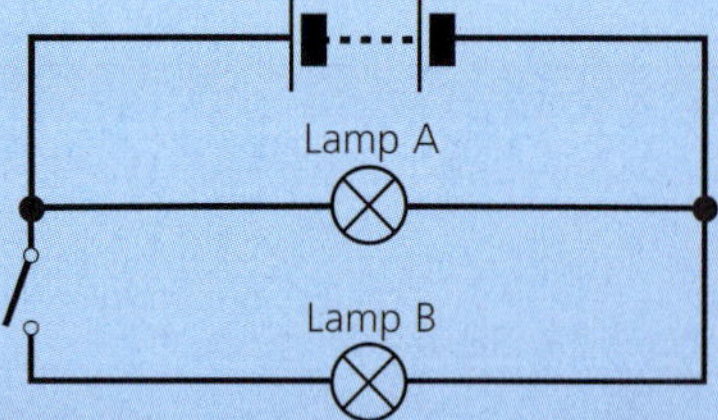

This is a parallel circuit. Lamp A will be on all the time, but lamp B will only come on when the switch is closed. Both lamps will be the same brightness.

You need to be able to apply the principles of basic electrical circuits to practical solutions.

Examples

In circuit 1, power from the battery flows through the gauge (on a car's dashboard) to a variable resistor. The variable resistor is controlled by a float that rides on the surface of the fuel in the tank. This float is always in contact with the variable resistor. When the fuel level is high, the float is high and so the resistance of the variable resistor is low. As the fuel level gets lower, the float gets lower and so the resistance of the variable resistor increases. The gauge on the dashboard inverts (reverses) the resistance of the variable resistor and displays it against a scale of E (empty) to F (full).

The low-fuel warning light is powered by a separate circuit (see circuit 2). Electricity flows from the battery through the light to a thermistor. A thermistor is like a switch. When it is submerged in fuel its resistance is very high; when it is in the air its resistance is very low. The thermistor is positioned near the bottom of the tank. When there is not much fuel left, the thermistor becomes exposed so its resistance falls to near zero. This allows current to flow through the circuit, which causes the light on the dashboard to light up.

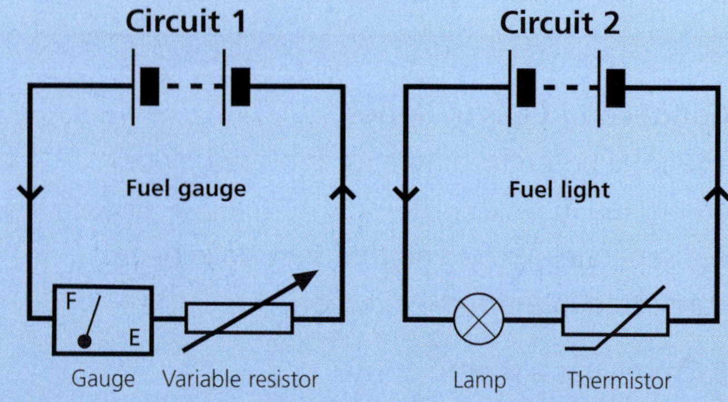

12.7

What is mains electricity and how can it be used safely?

Although useful, mains electricity can be very dangerous so it is important to know how to use it safely. To understand this, you need to know...

- what a direct current is
- what an alternating current is
- how electrical appliances are connected to the mains
- the structure and wiring of a three-pin plug
- the use of a circuit breaker, fuse and the earth wire.

Currents

A **direct current** (d.c.) always flows in the same direction. Cells and batteries supply direct current.

An **alternating current** (a.c.) changes the direction of flow back and forth continuously. The number of complete cycles of reversal per second is called the **frequency**, and for UK mains electricity this is 50 cycles per second (Hertz).

In the UK, the mains supply has a voltage of about 230 volts which, if it is not used safely, can kill.

The 3-Pin Plug

Most electrical appliances are connected to the mains electricity supply using a cable and a 3-pin plug which is inserted into a socket on the ring main circuit.

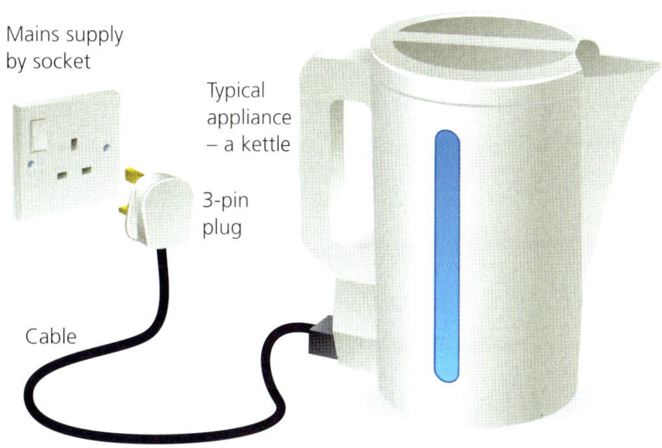

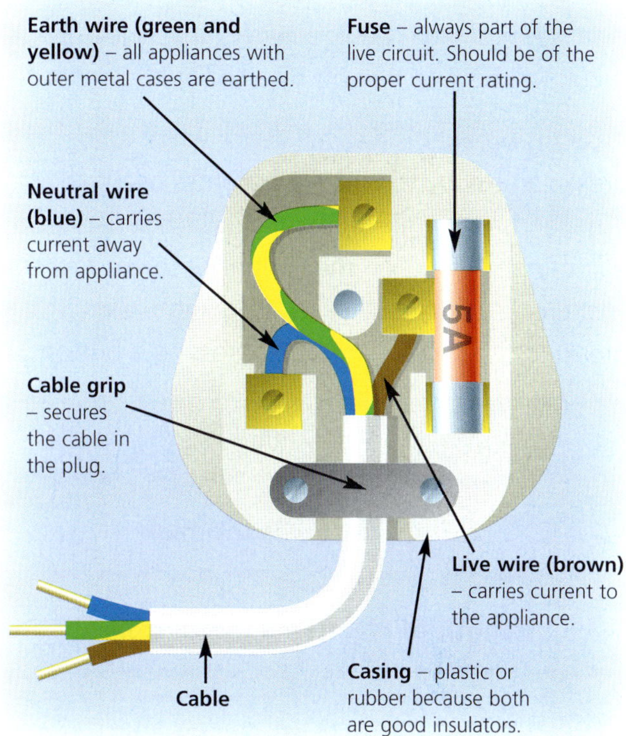

- The inner cores of the wires are made of copper because it is a good conductor.
- The outer layers are made of flexible plastic which is a good insulator.
- The pins of a plug are made from brass because it is a good conductor.

HT

The live terminal of the mains supply alternates between a positive and negative voltage with respect to the neutral terminal.

The neutral terminal stays at a voltage close to zero with respect to earth.

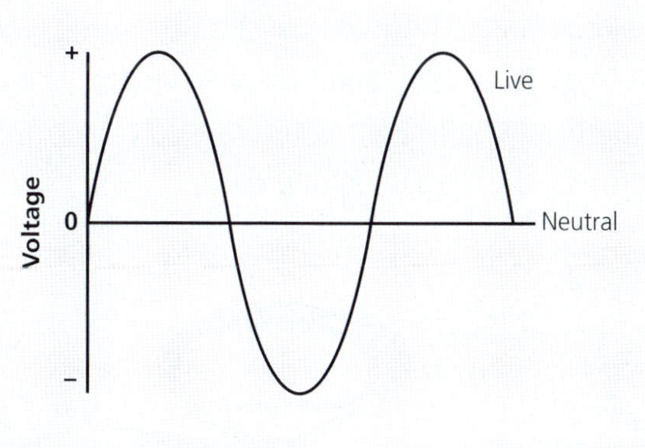

Unit 2

Circuit Breakers and Fuses

If an electrical fault causes a current that is too high, the circuit will be switched off by a circuit breaker or fuse.

A **circuit breaker** is a safety device which automatically breaks an electric circuit if it becomes overloaded. It depends on an electromagnet which separates a pair of contacts when the current becomes too high. This breaks the circuit (called 'tripping'). Circuit breakers can be easily reset by pressing a button.

A **fuse** is a short, thin piece of wire with a low melting point. When the current passing through it exceeds the current rating of the fuse, the fuse wire gets hot and melts or breaks, breaking the circuit. This prevents damage to the cable or the appliance that would be caused by overheating. The current rating of the fuse must be just above the normal working current of the appliance for the safety system to work properly.

A Circuit Breaker

- current becomes too high
- strength of electromagnet increases
- pair of contacts are pulled apart
- circuit is broken
- cable or appliance is protected

A Fuse

- current larger than current rating of fuse
- fuse wire melts
- circuit is broken
- no current flows
- cable or appliance is protected

Earthing

All electrical appliances with outer metal cases must be earthed. The outer case of an appliance is connected to the earth pin in the plug through the earth wire.

If a fault in the appliance connects the live wire to the case, the case will become **live.** The current will then 'run to earth' through the earth wire as this offers least resistance. This overload of current will cause the fuse to melt, or the circuit breaker to trip. Therefore, the earth wire and fuse work together to protect the appliance and user.

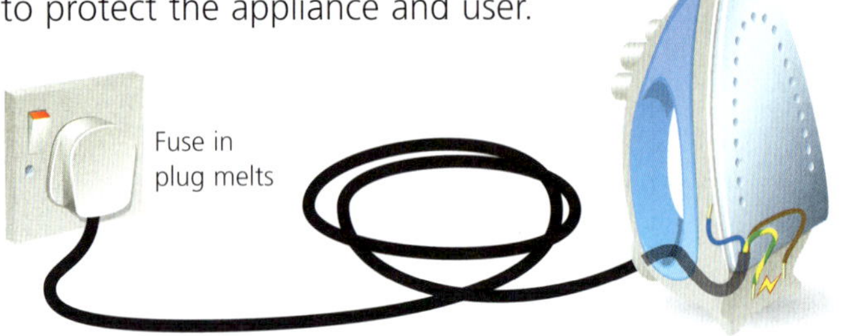

Earthing

- live casing
- short circuit
- current surges to earth
- fuse wire melts
- circuit is broken
- cable or appliance is protected

You need to be able to recognise errors in the wiring of a three-pin plug.

For safety reasons, it is very important that all plugs are wired correctly with no errors. Below are five examples of dangerously wired plugs.

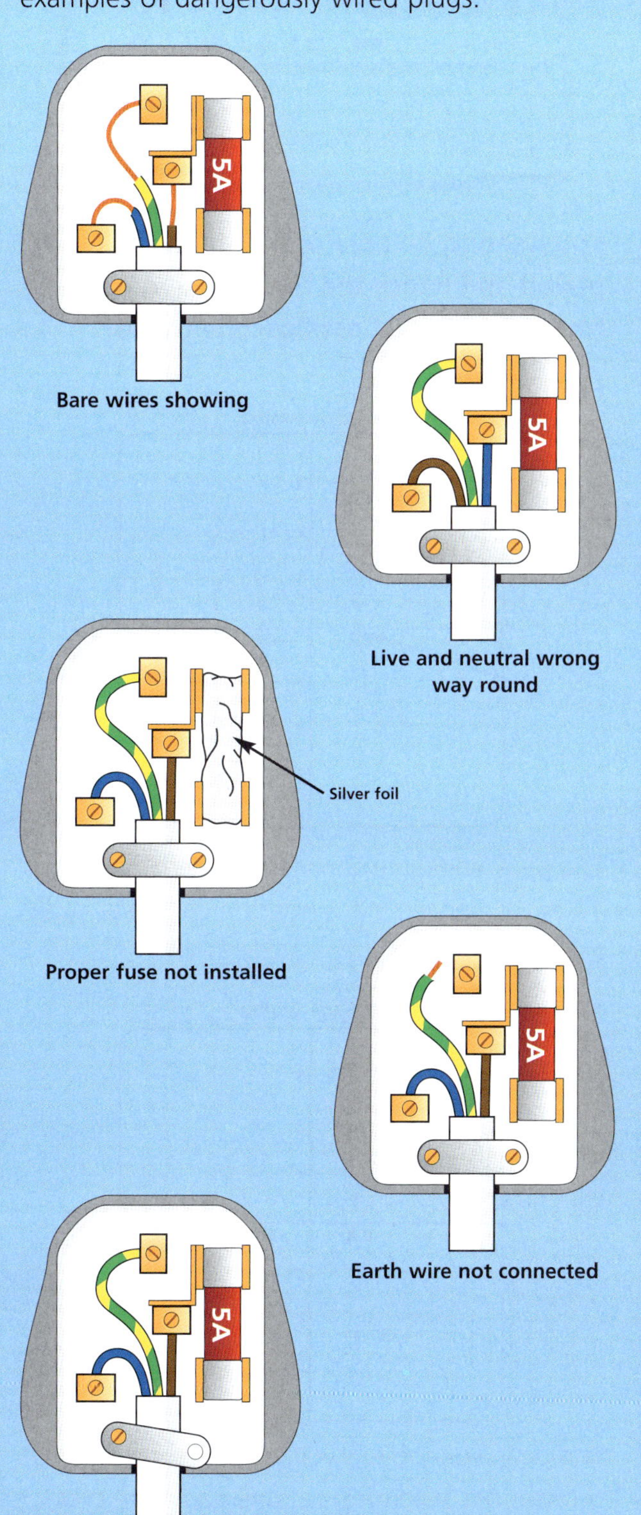

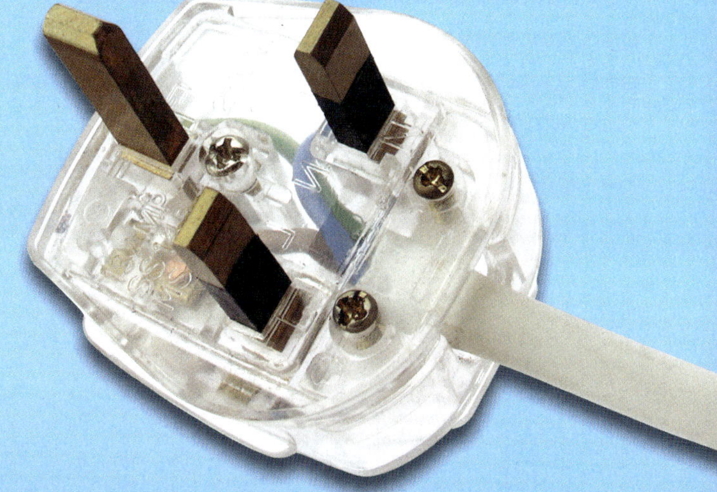

You need to be able to recognise dangerous practices in the use of mains electricity.

Apart from making sure that all plugs are wired correctly, there are some common-sense practices which should be followed at all times:

- replace all broken plugs and frayed cables
- keep plugs and cables away from water or heat
- never overload a socket with too many plugs
- make sure your hands are dry when switching appliances on or off.

How Science Works

You need to be able to compare potential differences (voltage) of d.c. supplies and the peak potential differences of a.c. supplies from diagrams of oscilloscope traces.

Frequency and voltage can be compared using an oscilloscope.

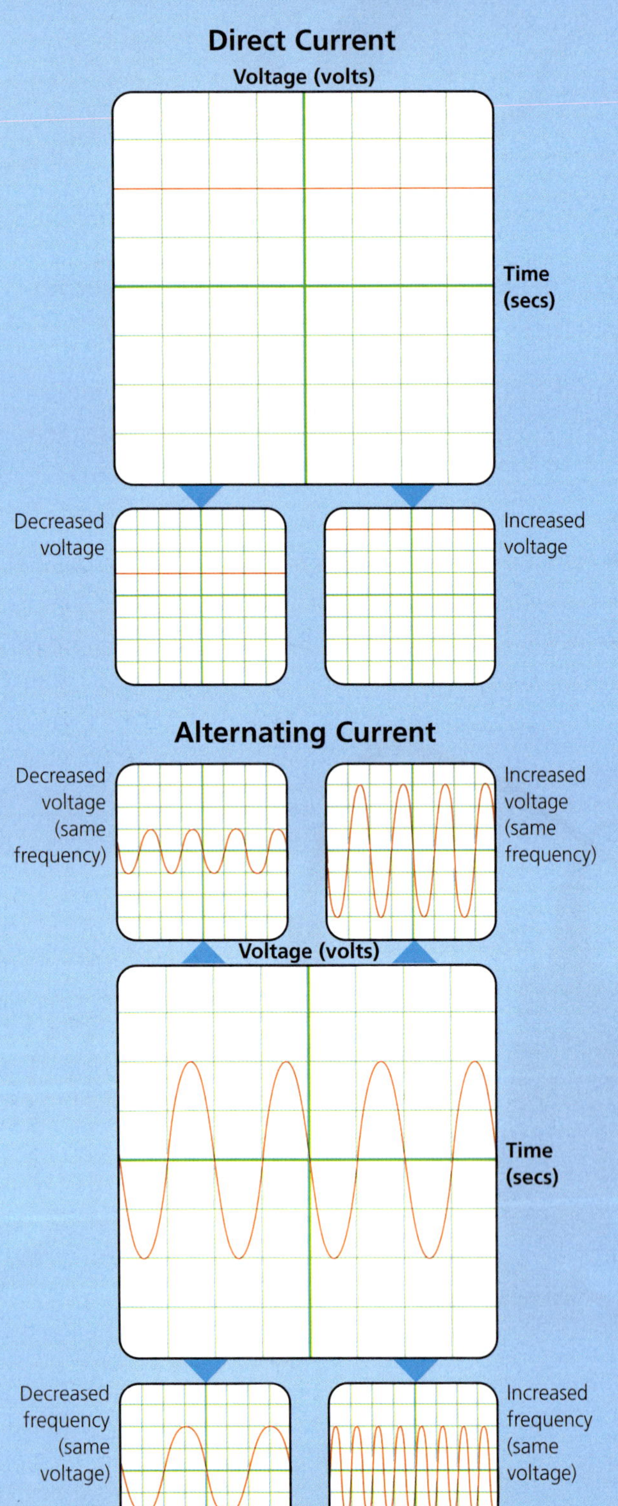

HT

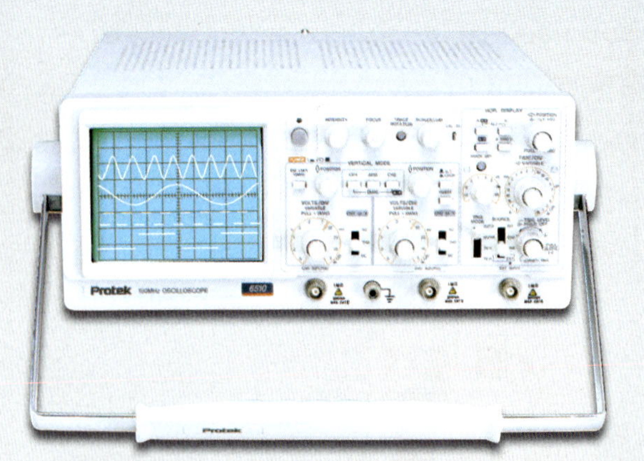

You need to be able to determine the period and hence the frequency of a supply from diagrams of oscilloscope traces.

Example

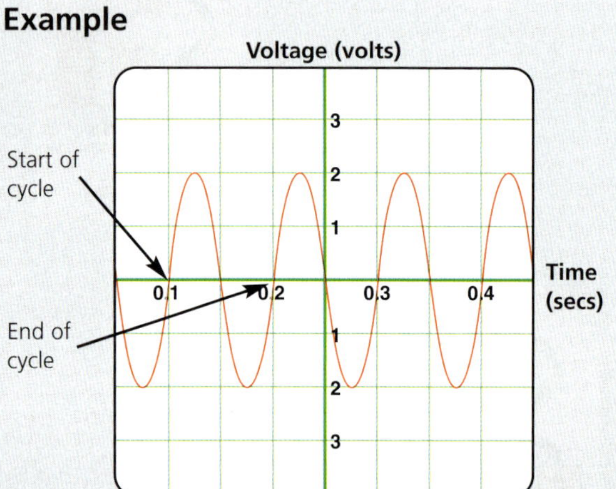

The peak voltage is 2 volts and the frequency is 10 cycles per second, since one complete cycle takes 0.1 seconds.

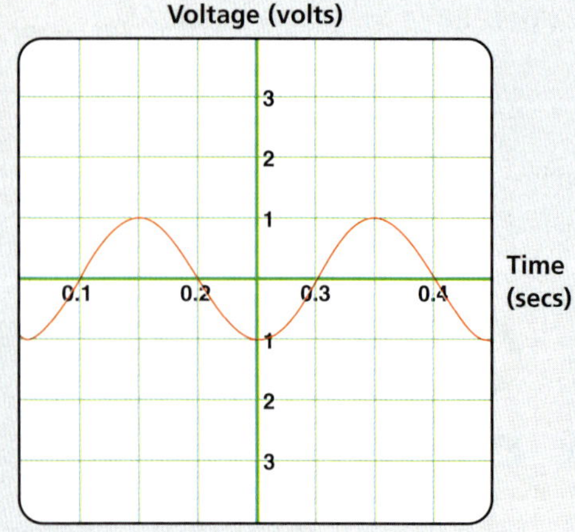

The peak voltage is 1 volt and the frequency is 5 cycles per second, since one complete cycle takes 0.2 seconds.

12.8

Why do we need to know the power of electrical appliances?

The power of an electrical appliance is the rate at which it transforms energy. If you know this and the potential difference, you can calculate the current and fuse needed for each appliance. To understand this, you need to know...

- what electric current is
- how to calculate power
- how power, potential difference and current are related
- the relationship between energy transformed, potential difference and charge
- how charge, current and time are related.

Power

An electric **current** is the flow of charge, which **transfers** electrical energy from a battery or power supply to components in a circuit. The rate of flow is measured in **amperes (A)**.

The components transform some of this electrical energy into other forms of energy, e.g. a resistor **transforms** electrical energy into heat energy. The rate at which energy is transformed in a device is called the **power**. This can be calculated using the formula...

Power (watt, W) = Energy transformed (joule, J) / Time (second, s)

Power can also be calculated using the formula...

Power (watt, W) = Potential difference (volt, V) x Current (amp, A)

where I is the current

P / V x I

Charge

The amount of electrical charge which passes any point in a circuit is measured in **coulombs (C)** and depends on the current that flows and the time taken.

Charge can be calculated using the formula:

Charge (coulomb, C) = Current (amp, A) x Time (second, s)

where Q is charge

Q / I x T

Example

If the circuit below is switched on for 40 seconds and the current is 0.5 amps, what is the charge?

Using the formula...

Charge = Current x Time

= 0.5A x 40s = **20 coulombs**

Transforming Energy

As the charge passes through a device, energy is transformed. The amount of energy transformed by every coulomb of charge depends on the size of the potential difference. The greater the potential difference, the more energy transformed by every coulomb of charge.

Energy transformed, potential difference and charge are related by the following formula...

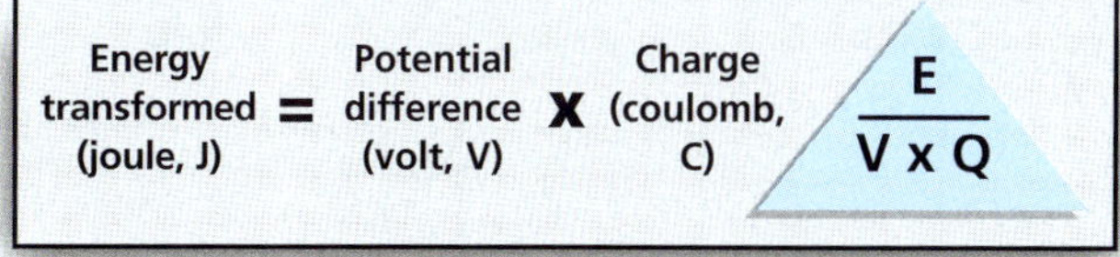

Energy transformed (joule, J) = Potential difference (volt, V) x Charge (coulomb, C)

E / V x Q

If the circuit alongside has a potential difference of 1.5V, how much energy is transformed?

Energy transformed = P.d. x Charge

= 1.5V x 20C = **30 joules**

Remember, the charge gained this energy from the supply voltage, i.e. the battery, which it transferred to the bulb in the 40 seconds the circuit was switched on.

How Science Works

You need to be able to calculate the current through an appliance from its power and the potential difference of the supply, and from this determine the size of the fuse needed.

When a new appliance is developed, the manufacturer needs to work out what size fuse it requires.

If the power and operating voltage (potential difference) are known, the current can be calculated by rearranging the power formula as follows:

$$\text{Current} = \frac{\text{Power}}{\text{Potential difference}}$$

Once the current has been calculated, the size of the fuse can then be determined. The fuse needs to be as close to the current as possible, but higher than it.

Fuses come in the following standard sizes: 1 amp, 3 amp, 7 amp, 13 amp, 20 amp, 25 amp and 30 amp.

Example

Device	Power	Voltage	Current	Ideal Fuse
Television	60W	230V	$\frac{60}{230}$ = 0.26A	3 amp
Oven	5500W	230V	$\frac{5500}{230}$ = 23.9A	25 amp
Computer	43W	16V	$\frac{43}{16}$ = 2.7A	3 amp
Drill	800W	240V	$\frac{800}{240}$ = 3.3A	5 amp
Microwave	1150W	230V	$\frac{1150}{230}$ = 5A	13 amp

12.9

What happens to radioactive substances when they decay?

We need to understand the structure of atoms in order to understand what happens to radioactive substances when they decay. To understand this, you need to know...

- the masses and relative charges of protons, neutrons and electrons
- what ions are
- what isotopes are
- what the mass number represents
- what effect alpha and beta decay have on radioactive nuclei
- the origins of background radiation.

Atoms

An atom is made up of three parts: protons, neutrons and electrons.

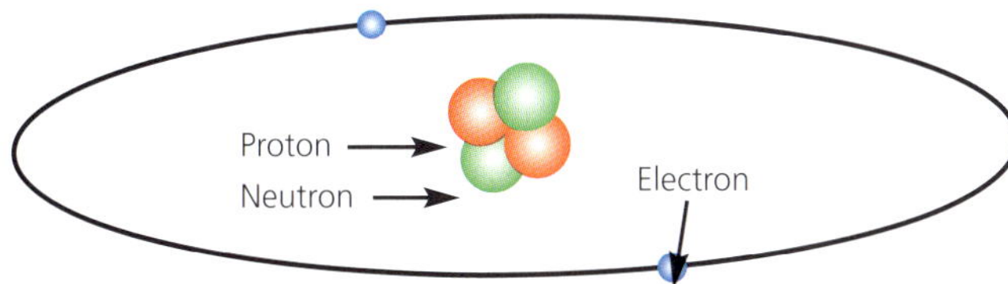

Atomic Particle	Relative Mass	Relative Charge
Proton	1	+1
Neutron	1	0
Electron	0 (nearly)	-1

An atom has the same number of protons as electrons so the atom as a whole has no electrical charge.

All atoms of a particular element have the same number of protons. Atoms of different elements have different numbers of protons. The number of protons defines the element.

The number of protons and neutrons in an atom is called its **mass number**. The total number of protons in an atom is called its **atomic number**.

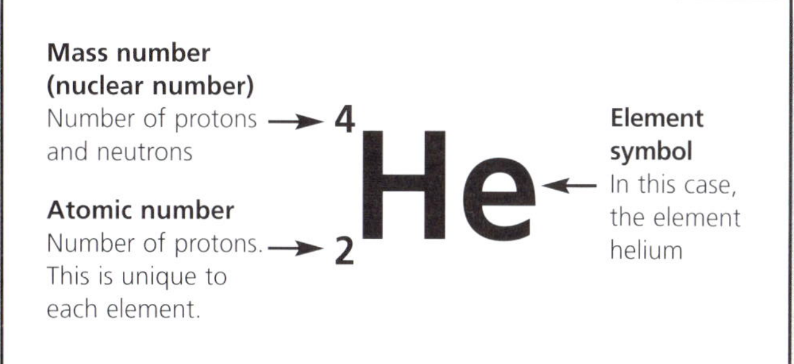

However, some atoms of the same element can have different numbers of neutrons. These are called **isotopes**.

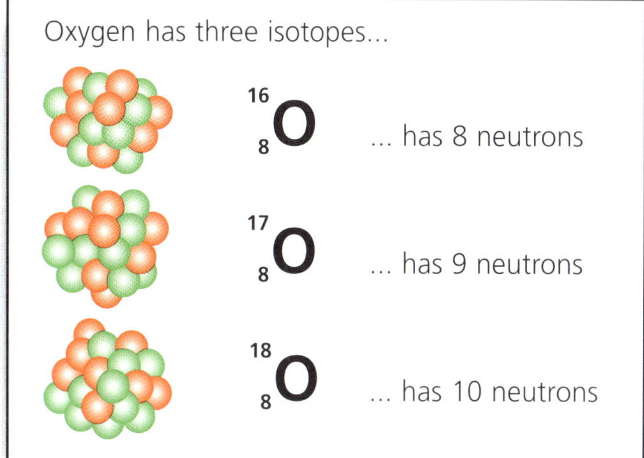

Radioactive Decay

Radioactive isotopes (radioisotopes or radionuclides) are atoms with unstable nuclei which may disintegrate and emit radiation. This is **radioactive decay** which results in the formation of a different atom with a different number of protons.

Alpha (α) Decay

The original atom decays by ejecting an alpha (α) particle from the nucleus. This particle is a helium nucleus: a particle made up of two protons and two neutrons. A new atom is formed with α decay.

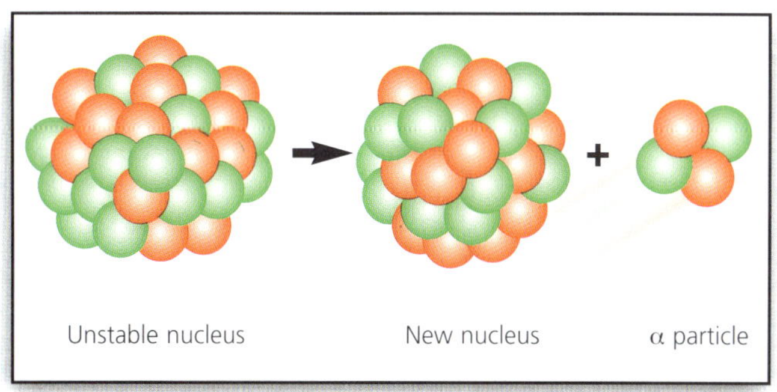

Radioactive Decay (cont.)

Beta (β) Decay

The original atom decays by changing a neutron into a proton and an electron. This high energy electron which is now ejected from the nucleus is a beta (β) particle. A new atom is formed with β decay.

There is another type of radiation – gamma (γ) radiation. However, unlike alpha and beta, gamma emissions have no effect on the structure of the nucleus.

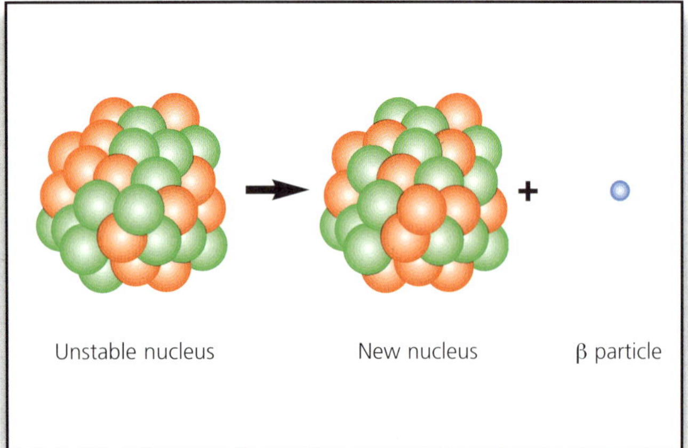

Ionisation

When radioactive particles collide with neutral atoms or molecules they may become charged due to electrons being knocked out of their structure.

This alters their structure leaving them as charged particles called **ions**. Alpha and beta radiation are therefore known as ionising radiation and can damage molecules in healthy cells, which results in the death of the cell.

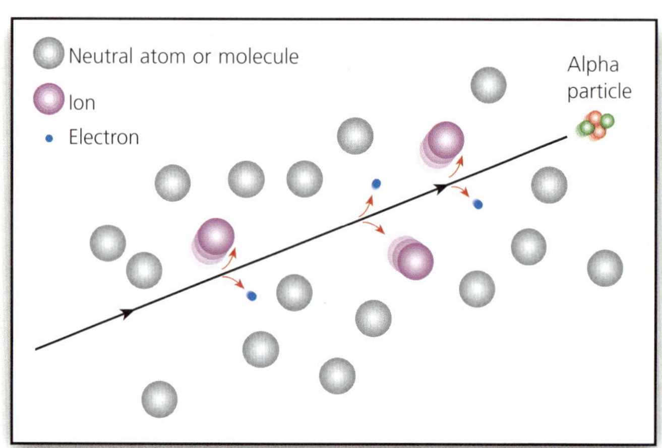

Background Radiation

Radiation occurs naturally all around us. This is known as background radiation. It only provides a very small dose altogether so there is no danger to our health.

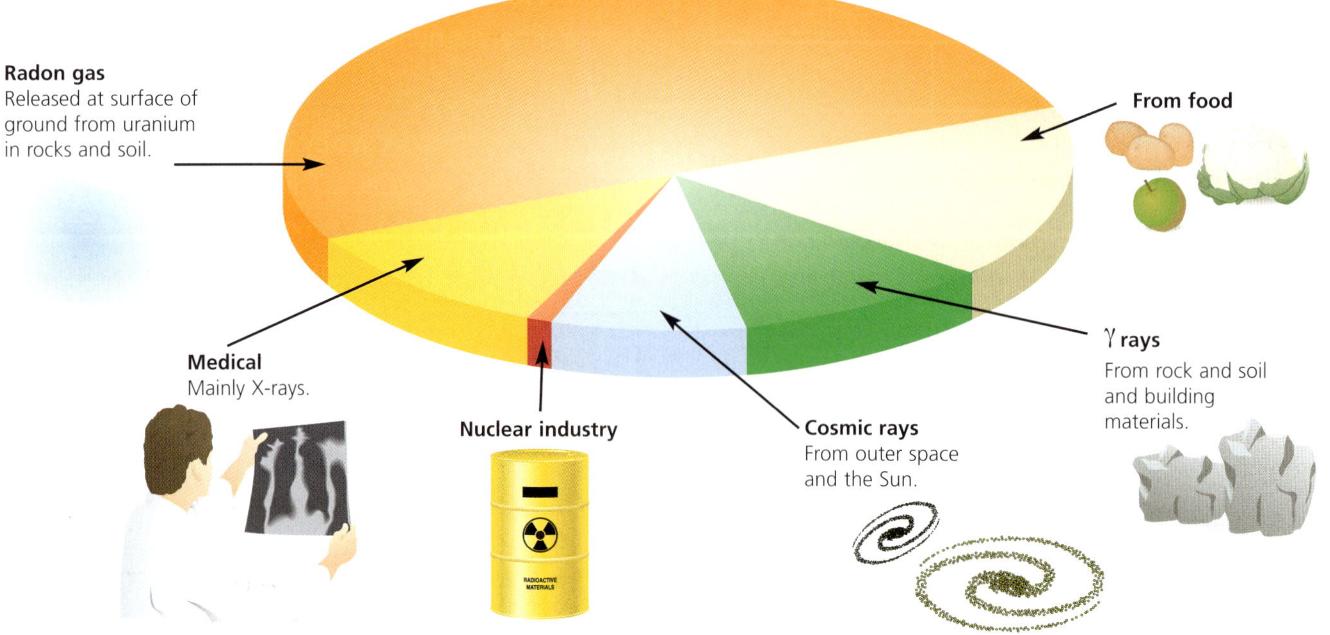

HT **You need to be able to explain how the Rutherford and Marsden scattering experiment led to the 'plum pudding' model of the atom being replaced by the nuclear model.**

In 1879, J.J. Thomson, a physicist, reasoned that since electrons were responsible for only a very small proportion of an atom's mass, they would take up an equally small proportion of an atom's size. He proposed that an atom consisted of a positive sphere of matter in which negative electrons were embedded.

The resulting model looked rather like a plum pudding, so it was therefore known as the 'plum pudding' model of the atom.

However, this model was disproved in 1911 by Ernest Rutherford, a British physicist, when he designed the gold foil scattering experiment.

Rutherford placed a thin piece of gold foil in the centre of a circular chamber lined with zinc sulfide. A radioactive source emitting alpha particles was focused on the gold foil target and the results were observed through a microscope.

Most alpha particles were seen to pass straight through the gold foil; this would indicate that the gold atoms were composed of large amounts of open space. However, some particles were deflected slightly and a few even bounced back towards the source. This would indicate that the alpha particles passed close to something positively charged within the atom and were repelled by it.

These observations brought Rutherford to conclude that...

- gold atoms, and therefore all atoms, consist largely of empty space with a small, dense positive core. He called this core the **nucleus**
- the nucleus is positively charged
- the electrons are arranged around the nucleus with a great deal of space between them.

This is called the **nuclear atomic model.**

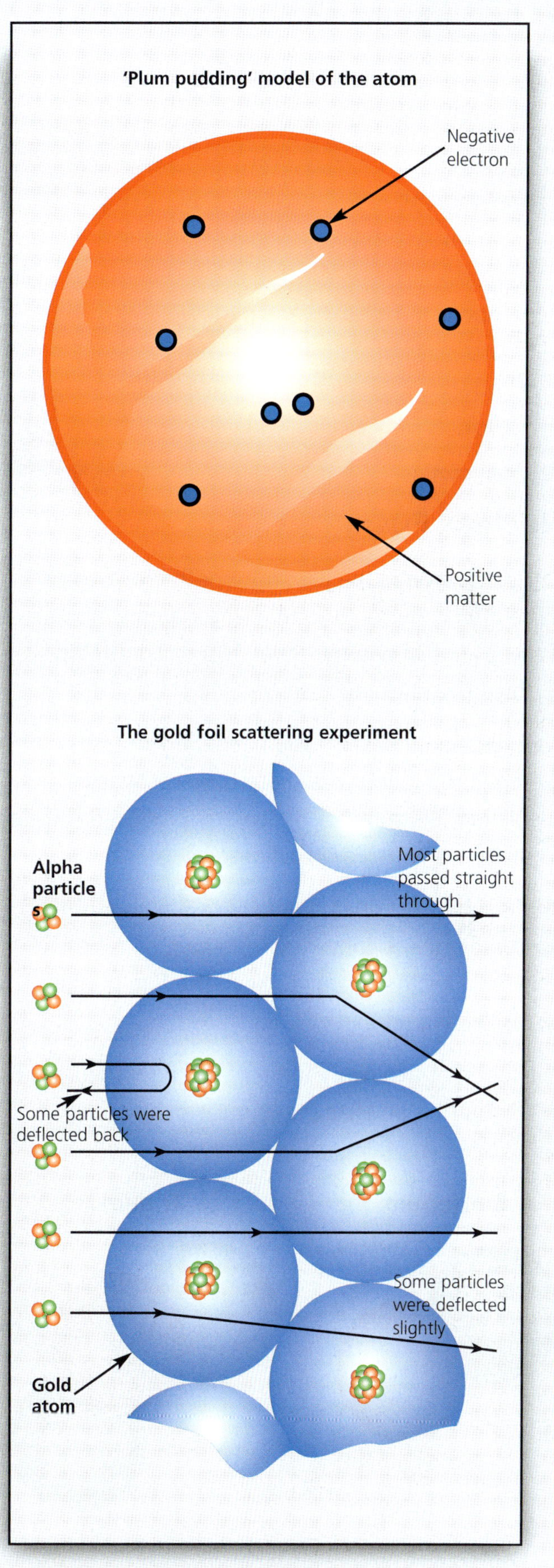

12.10

What are nuclear fission and nuclear fusion?

Nuclear fission is the splitting of atomic nuclei whilst nuclear fusion is the joining together of atomic nuclei. To understand this, you need to know...

- how uranium-235 and plutonium-239 are used
- how a chain reaction can be created
- how energy is released in stars.

Nuclear Fusion

Nuclear **fusion** is the **joining** together of two or more atomic nuclei to form a larger atomic nucleus. It takes a lot of energy – over 100 million Kelvin – to force the nuclei to fuse.

As a reaction, nuclear fusion generally releases more energy than it uses, which makes it self-sustaining, i.e. some of the energy produced is used to drive further fusion reactions.

This is how stars release energy. In the core of the Sun, hydrogen is converted to helium by fusion. This provides the energy to keep the Sun burning and allow life on Earth.

The fusion of two heavy forms of hydrogen (deuterium and tritium) is an example of nuclear fusion.

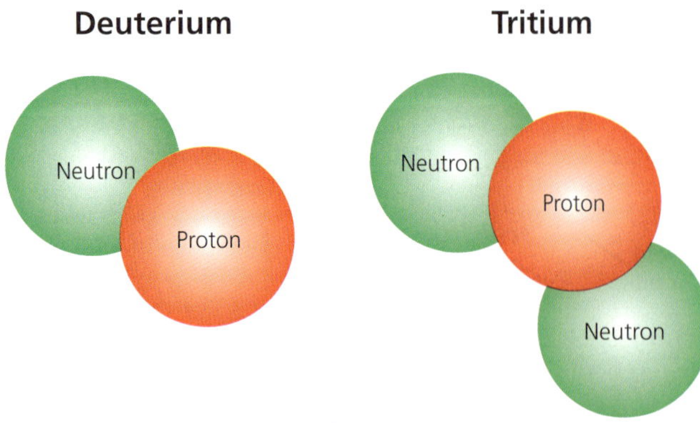

When they are forced together, the deuterium and tritium nuclei fuse together to form a new helium atom and an unchanged neutron.

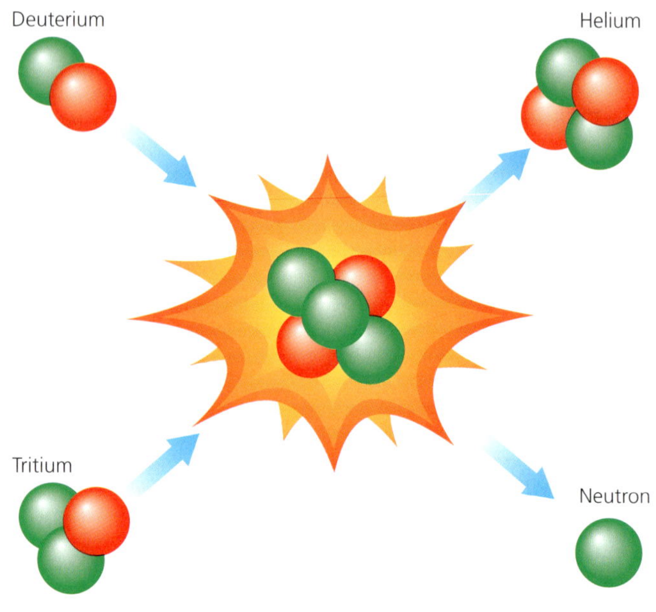

Nuclear Fission

Nuclear **fission** is the process of **splitting** atomic nuclei. It is used in nuclear reactors to produce energy to make electricity. The two substances commonly used are uranium-235 and plutonium-239.

The products of nuclear fission are radioactive and there are dangers with regard to the reaction getting out of control (e.g. Chernobyl). However, the amount of energy released by an atom during nuclear fission, or radioactive disintegration, is much greater than the energy released when a chemical bond is made between two atoms.

On a Small Scale

A uranium atom must first absorb a neutron before fission can take place. When a neutron collides with a very large nucleus (e.g. uranium) the nucleus splits up into two smaller nuclei (e.g. barium and krypton). This releases energy and new neutrons.

On a Large Scale

The new neutrons can each cause a new fission; this is a chain reaction (i.e. it carries on and on and on...).

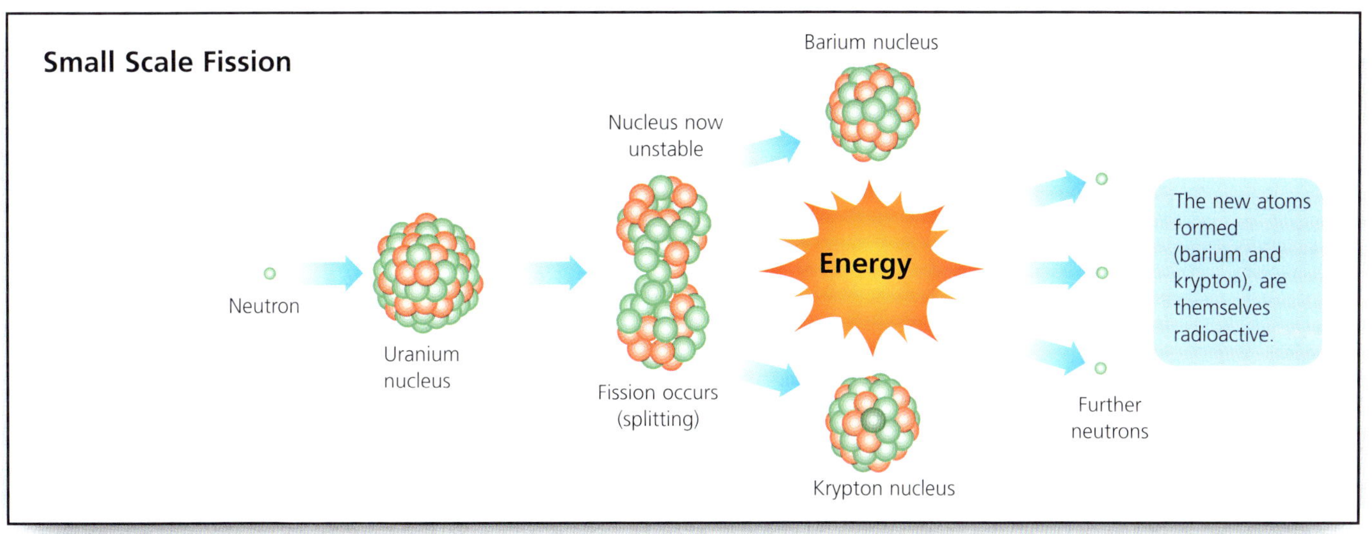

Large Scale Fission

Energy

Energy

Energy

Energy

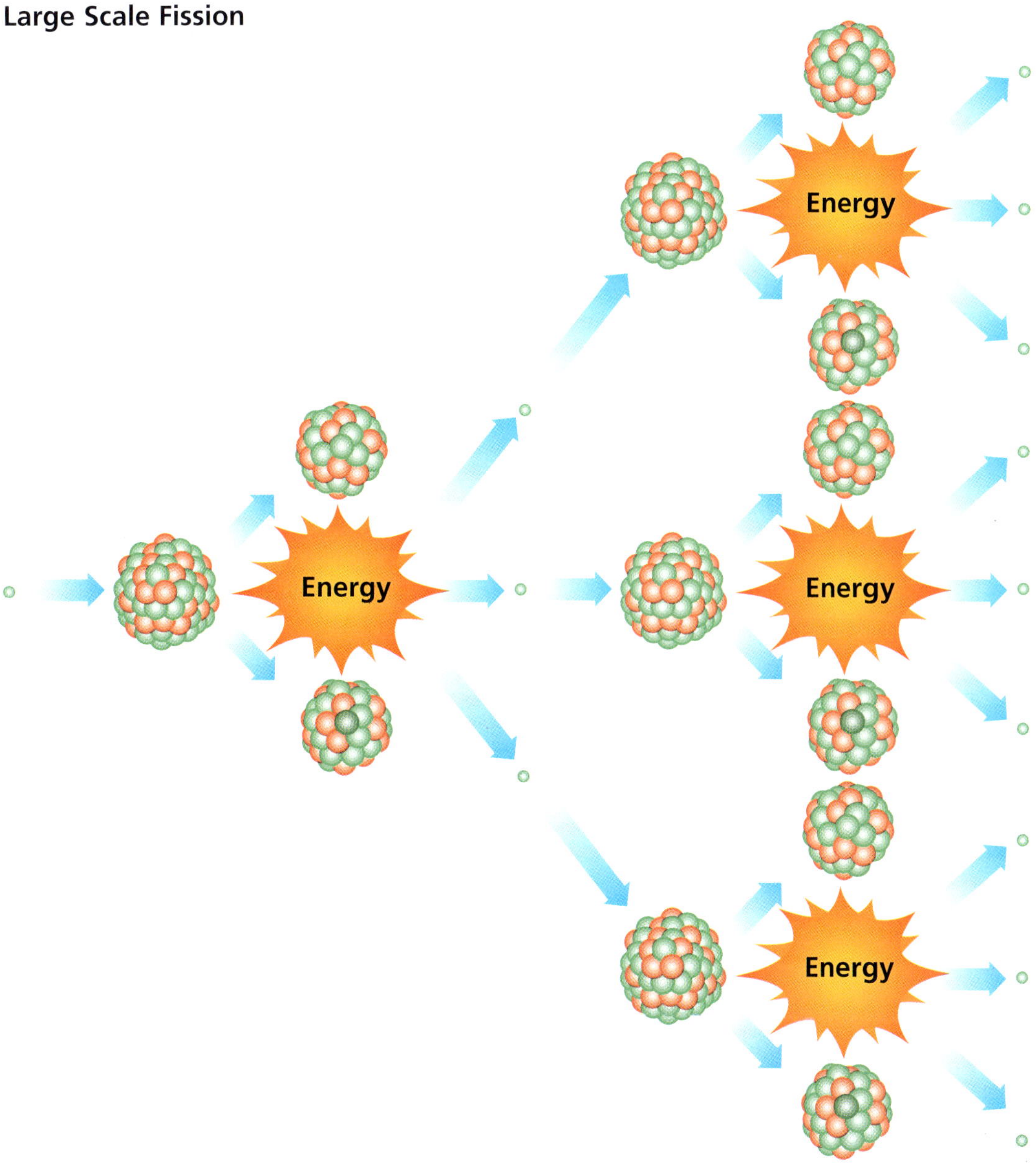

The energy is released in the form of heat. Each fission reaction only produces a tiny amount of energy, but there are billions and billions of reactions every second.

Example Questions

For Unit 2, you will have to complete one written paper with structured questions.

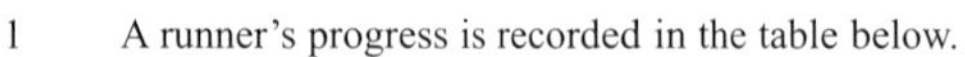

1 A runner's progress is recorded in the table below.

Time (mins)	5	10	15	20	25	30
Total distance (km)	1	2	3	3	4	5

(a) Plot the runner's journey on the distance–time graph below and connect the points using straight lines.

2

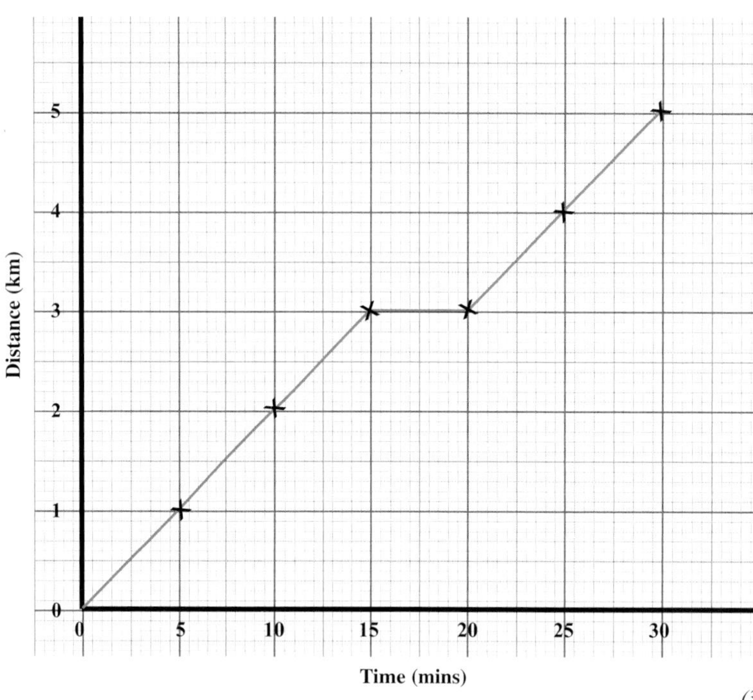

(3 marks)

(b) How far did the runner travel in total?

3 5km.

(1 mark)

(c) For how long did the runner remain stationary?

4 5 minutes.

(1 mark)

(d) What was the runner's average speed?

5 10km/h.

(1 mark)

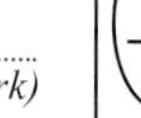

6

1. Read the information carefully to make sure you understand what the data in a table shows before answering any questions.
2. Make sure you plot data accurately and neatly, otherwise you might get subsequent questions wrong!
3. Don't forget to include units (e.g. km) in your answers.
4. In a distance–time graph, a flat horizontal line means the object is not moving.
5. Average speed = $\frac{\text{Distance (km)}}{\text{Time (hours)}} = \frac{5}{0.5} = 10\text{km/h}$

Key Words

Acceleration – the rate at which a body increases in speed
Alternating current (ac) – an electric current which changes direction of flow continuously
Attraction – the drawing together of two materials with different types of charges
Charged – having an overall positive or negative electric charge
Circuit breaker – a safety device which breaks an electric circuit automatically when it becomes overloaded
Current – the rate of flow of an electrical charge, measured in amperes (A)
Diode – an electrical device that allows current to flow in one direction
Direct current (dc) – an electric current which flows in one direction
Distance – the space between two points
Distance–time graph – represents speed (distance travelled against time taken)
Electron – a negatively charged subatomic particle
Electrostatic – producing or caused by static electricity
Energy – the capacity of a physical system to do work; measured in joules (J)
Force – a push or pull acting upon an object
Friction – the resistive force between two surfaces as they move over each other
Fuse – a thin piece of metal which overheats and melts to break an electric circuit if it is overloaded
Ion – a charged particle formed when an atom gains or loses electrons
Isotopes – atoms of the same element but with a different number of neutrons
Joule – a measure of energy and work done
Kinetic energy – the energy possessed by an object due to its movement
Mass – the quantity of matter in an object
Momentum – a measure of the state of motion of an object as a product of its mass and velocity
Newton – a measure of force
Neutron – a neutrally charged subatomic particle
Nuclear fission – the splitting of atomic nuclei
Nuclear fusion – the joining together of atomic nuclei
Parallel circuit – a circuit where there are two (or more) paths for the current to take
Potential difference (p.d.) / voltage – the difference in electrical charge between two charged points
Proton – a positively charged subatomic particle
Repulsion – the pushing away of two materials with the same type of charge
Resistance – opposition to the flow of an electric current
Resistor – an electrical device that resists the flow of an electric current
Series circuit – a circuit where there is one path for the current to take
Speed – the rate at which an object moves
Static electricity – electricity produced by friction
Terminal velocity – the maximum velocity reached by a falling object (gravitational force is equal to the frictional forces acting on it)
Thermistor – a resistor whose resistance varies greatly with temperature
Transfer – to move energy from one place to another
Transform – to change energy from one form into another, e.g. electrical energy to heat energy
Velocity – the speed at which an object moves in a particular direction
Velocity–time graph – represents acceleration (velocity against time taken)
Voltage / potential difference (p.d.) – the difference in electrical charge between two charged points
Weight – the gravitational force exerted upon an object
Work – the energy transfer that occurs when a force causes an object to move a certain distance

13.1

How do forces have a turning effect?

Balanced forces acting on a body can make the body turn but not change speed. To understand this, you need to know...

- what a moment is and how to calculate it
- what a body's centre of mass is
- what factors affect the stability of a body
- how a body becomes unbalanced.

Moments

Forces can be used to turn objects about a pivot. The turning effect of a force is called the **moment**. If a spanner was used to unscrew a wheel nut, it would exert a moment, or turning force, on the nut.

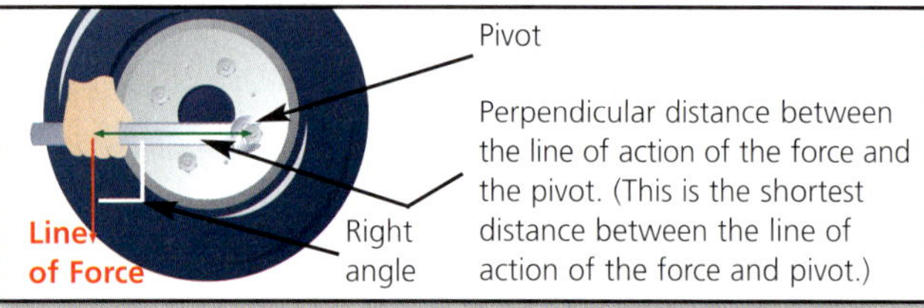

The size of the moment is given by the equation:

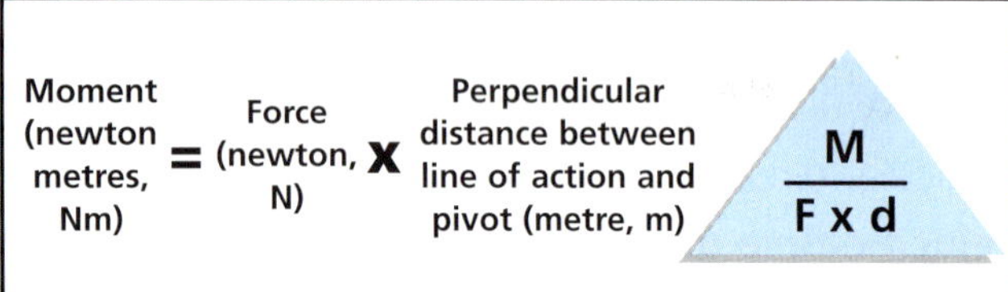

There are two ways of increasing the moment or turning force. You can...

- increase the force applied
- increase the perpendicular distance between the line of action of the force and the pivot.

Example

In the diagram above, the man exerts a force of 120N and the perpendicular distance from his hand to the pivot is 15cm. What moment does he exert?

Using the formula...

Moment (Nm) = Force (N) x Perpendicular distance between line of action and pivot (m)

= 120N x 0.15m

= **18Nm**

Centre of Mass

The **centre of mass** (C of M) of an object is the point through which the whole weight (W) of the object acts. If you were to balance an object on the end of your finger, the point at which the object balances is the centre of mass. The centre of mass of a symmetrical object is found along the axis of symmetry.

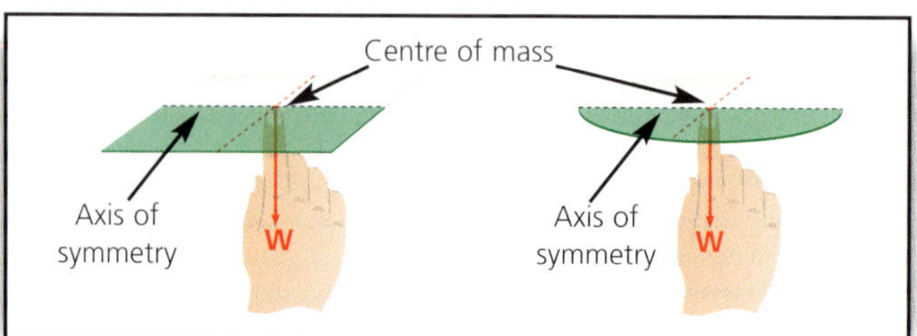

Finding the Centre of Mass

When an object is suspended, it will always come to rest with its centre of mass situated directly below the point of suspension. In this position, the force (weight of the object) does not exert any turning force on the object since it is directly below the pivot (point of suspension). If the object is then suspended from a different point of suspension, the centre of mass will be at the point where the two lines cross.

To find the centre of mass of a sheet of material...

1. hang the sheet and a plumbline from one point so both are free to rotate, and mark the position of the plumbline as a vertical line
2. repeat with the sheet and plumbline hanging at a different position and mark the position of the second plumbline
3. check the position of the centre of mass by balancing the sheet on the end of your finger at the point where the two lines cross. If you have found the centre of mass correctly, the sheet will balance on the end of your finger.

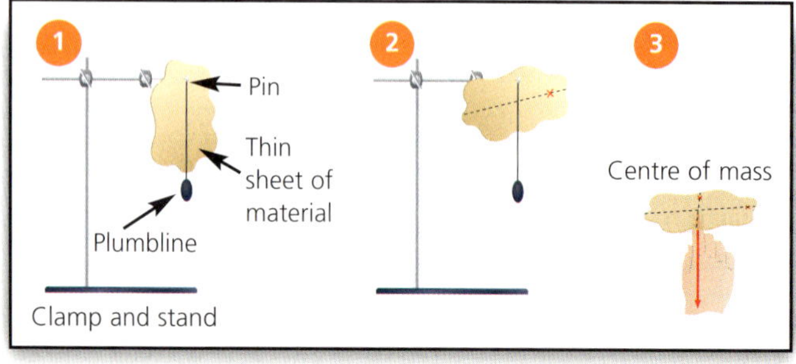

Law Of Moments

When an object is not turning, or is balanced, the total moments of the forces tending to turn the object in a clockwise direction are exactly balanced by the total moments of the forces tending to turn the object in an anticlockwise direction.

Total clockwise moments = Total anticlockwise moments

The plank below is pivoted at its centre of mass, and is supporting two forces pulling downwards, F_1 and F_2.

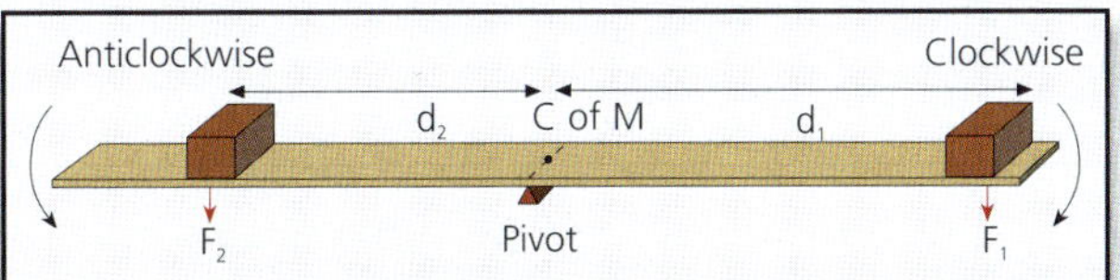

Since the object is balanced…

Total clockwise moments = Total anticlockwise moments

$$F_1 \times d_1 = F_2 \times d_2.$$

Example 1

The diagram shows the forces acting on a balanced object. It is pivoted at its centre of mass. Calculate F_2.

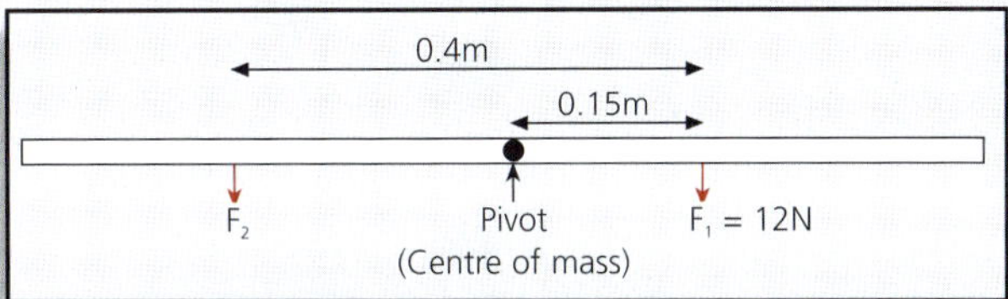

Since the object is balanced…

Total clockwise moments = Total anticlockwise moments

$$12N \times 0.15m = F_2 \times (0.4 - 0.15)m$$

$$\text{Therefore, } F_2 = \frac{12N \times 0.15m}{0.25m}$$

$$= \mathbf{7.2N}$$

Example 2

The diagram shows the forces acting on a balanced object. Calculate the weight of the object.

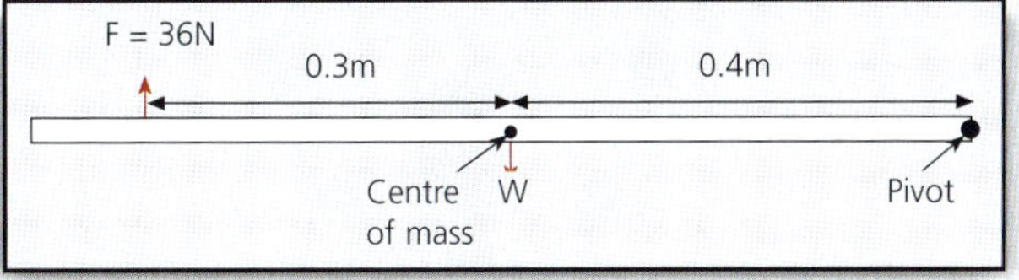

An important point to note is that the object is not pivoted at its centre of mass. The weight of the object exerts a turning force in an anticlockwise direction.

Since the object is balanced…

Total clockwise moments = Total anticlockwise moments

$$36N \times (0.3 + 0.4)m = W \times 0.4m$$

$$\text{Therefore, } W = \frac{36N \times 0.7m}{0.4m}$$

$$= \mathbf{63N}$$

Stability

Any object will topple over if the line of action of its weight (the force) lies outside its base; the weight of the object causes a turning effect and the object will tend to fall over.

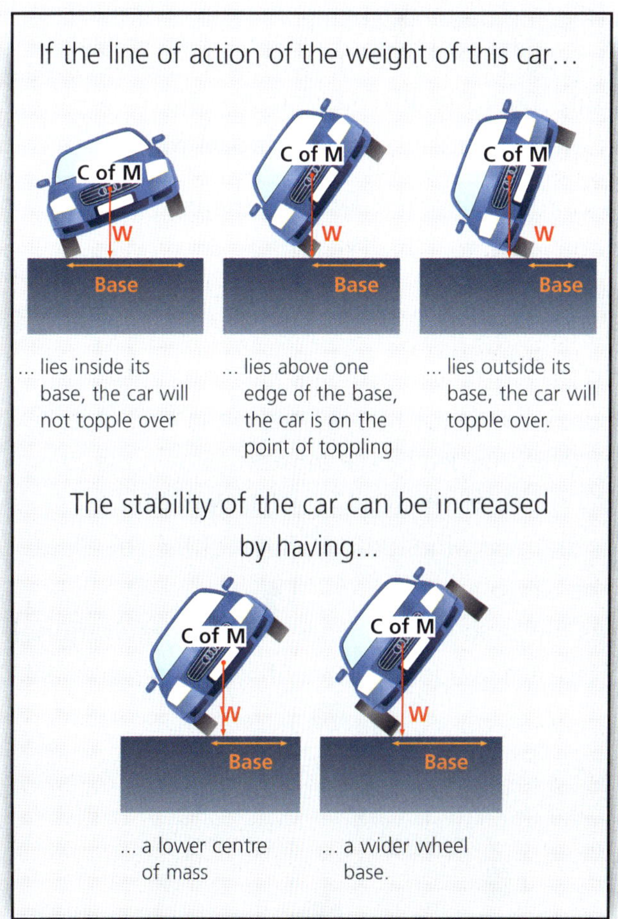

This is why racing cars have a low centre of mass *and* a wide wheel base.

13.2

What keeps bodies moving in a circle?

A balanced force can keep a body moving in a straight line or make it remain stationary. For a body to move in a circular path, the force acting on it must be constantly unbalanced. To understand this, you need to know...

- about acceleration in a circle
- what centripetal force is
- what factors cause centripetal force to increase.

Motion in a Circle

Many objects move in circular, or near circular paths. For example: a rubber ball being spun round on a piece of string; spinning rides at fairgrounds; a car turning; the Earth and other planets in orbit around the Sun.

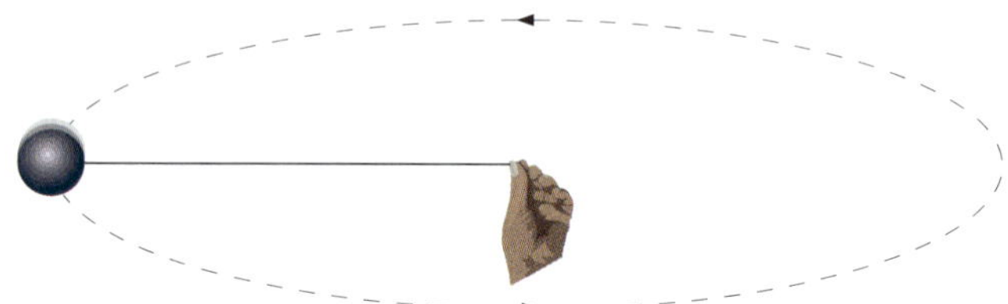

Centripetal Force

When an object moves in a circle it continuously accelerates towards the centre of the circle. This acceleration does not change the speed of the object, but the direction of its motion, i.e. its velocity. The resultant force causing this acceleration is called the **centripetal force.**

The word 'centripetal' describes the direction of the force, i.e. towards the centre of the circle (inwards). There are several different forces that can act in this way.

- In the case of the whirling ball, the centripetal force that keeps the ball moving in its circular path is provided by the **tension** force in the string.
- As a car makes a turn, the **frictional** force acting upon the turned wheels of the car allow the car to turn.
- As the Earth orbits the Sun, it is the **gravitational** force acting upon the Earth that causes it to rotate.

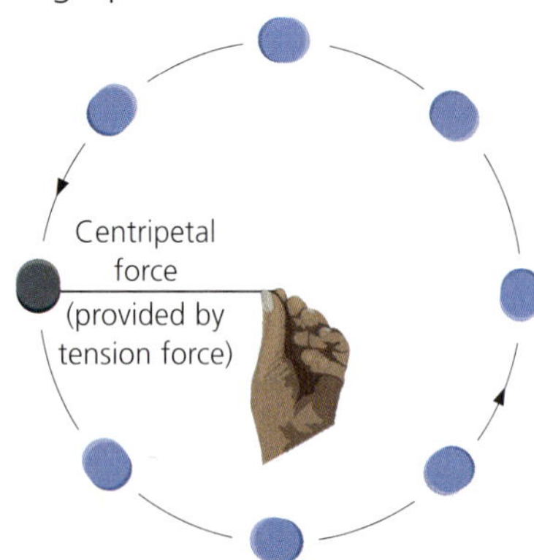

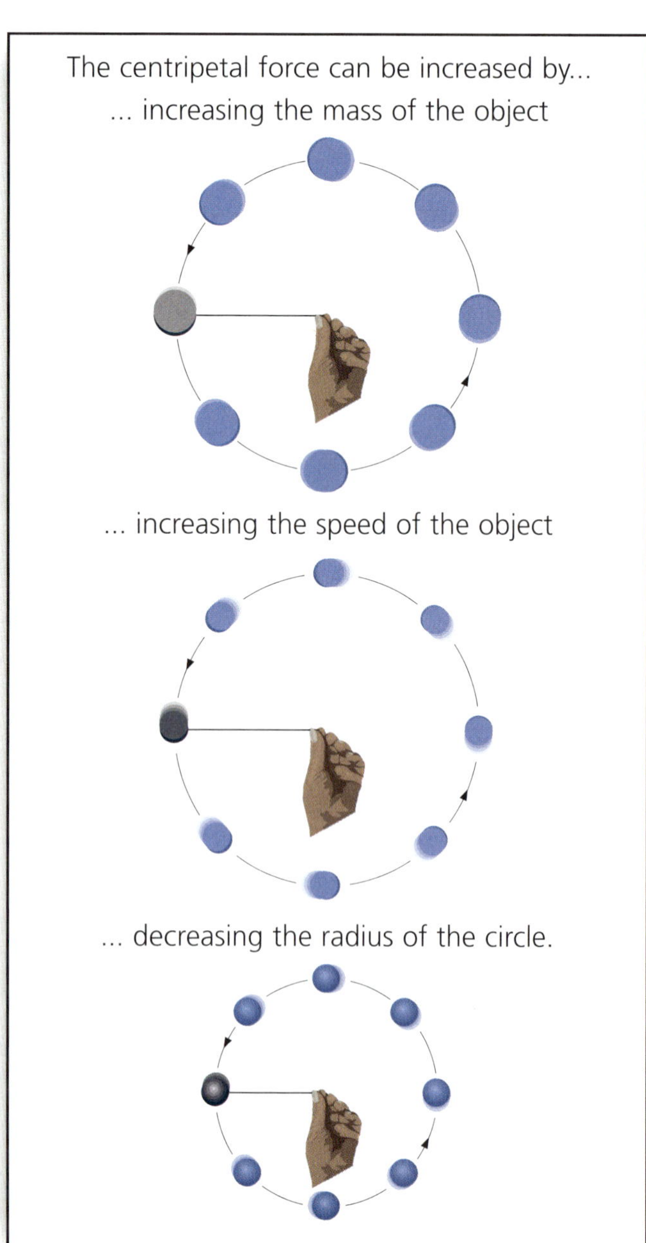

13.3

What provides the centripetal force for planets and satellites?

Planets orbit the Sun and artificial satellites orbit the Earth. These objects are kept in orbit by gravitational force, which provides centripetal force. To understand this, you need to know...

- about gravity and its effect on objects
- what factors cause gravity to increase
- how objects stay in their orbit
- why different orbits are used for different satellites.

Gravity and our Solar System

The Earth, Sun, Moon and all other objects attract each other with a force called **gravity**. The bigger the mass of the object, the bigger the force of gravity.

The orbit of any planet is an ellipse (slightly squashed circle) with the Sun at one focus. It is gravitational force that provides the centripetal force that maintains the elliptical orbits of planets and satellites.

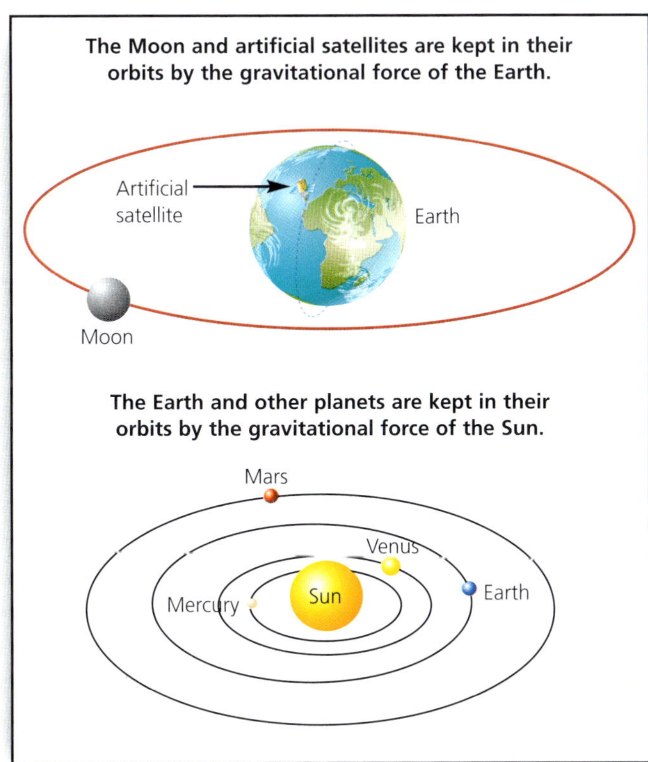

Gravity and Orbiting Speed

As the distance between two bodies increases, there is a proportionally greater decrease in the force of gravity between them.

If the distance between two objects is doubled, the force between them becomes $\frac{1}{4}$ of the original force. Trebling the distance results in $\frac{1}{9}$ of the force.

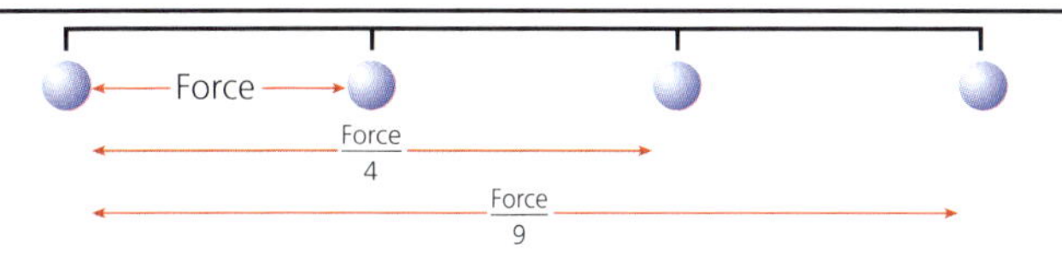

This means that in order to stay in orbit at a particular distance, objects must orbit at a particular speed; this balances the gravitational force. So, satellites further away orbit slowly and take a much longer time to complete an orbit (as the circumference is much larger).

Artificial Satellites

Communications Satellites link up different countries so that radio, TV broadcasts and telephone calls can be sent from one country to another.

A geostationary communications satellite has a geostationary orbit. This means it passes high above the equator moving around the Earth at exactly the same rate as the Earth spins, i.e. it takes 24 hours to complete its orbit, so it always stays at the same point above the equator. Potential interference with each other's signals means that there is only room for about 400 of these satellites.

Monitoring Satellites collect information about the atmosphere, including movement of clouds, so that weather forecasts can be made.

A polar monitoring satellite has a low polar orbit, i.e. it passes continuously over the North and South poles, so that the Earth spins beneath it. These satellites orbit and scan the Earth several times every day from a much closer range than a geostationary satellite.

How Science Works

You need to be able to interpret data on planets and satellites moving in orbits that approximate to circular paths.

Example 1

The following planets orbit a star in a distant galaxy.

Planet	Time Taken to Complete One Orbit (hrs)
Azron	236
Zanthon	49
Xelta	26
Pynda	52
Razid	120

Arrange the planets in order according to their distance from the star, with the closest first.

The further away an orbiting body is, the greater the distance it has to travel, so the longer it takes to complete an orbit. Therefore, the correct answer to this question would be…
Xelta, Zanthon, Pynda, Razid, Azron.

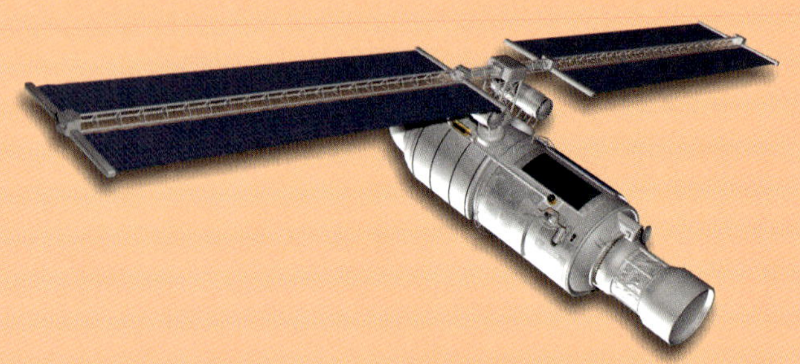

Example 2

Astronomy News, Star Charts, Space Pictures

Apple .Mac Amazon eBay Yahoo! News

MONITORING WEATHER

The following weather satellites are in orbit around Earth.

Identify whether each satellite is in geostationary orbit or polar orbit.

Satellite	Time taken to orbit the Earth	Average height above the Earth
TIROS	85 minutes	475km
Climsat	175 minutes	890km
Meteosat	24 hours	36 000km

Satellites in polar orbits follow a path that passes over the north and south poles. This means the Earth spins beneath them and they can scan the planet several times a day. TIROS and Climsat orbit the Earth in less than 24 hours so they are in polar orbit.

Geostationary satellites follow the line of the equator at the same rate. They remain above the same spot on the planet by moving at the same speed as the earth spins (one revolution in 24 hours). Meteosat takes 24 hours to complete an orbit so it is in geostationary orbit.

13.4

What do mirrors and lenses do to light?

Mirrors and lenses with a uniform curvature can be used to form images in optical devices such as cameras and magnifying glasses.
To understand this, you need to know...

- that the angle of incidence is equal to the angle of reflection
- how an image is defined
- the nature of images produced by a plane, concave and convex mirror
- how light is refracted at an interface and a prism
- the nature of images produced by a diverging and a converging lens.

Reflection of Light

When light strikes a surface it changes direction; it is **reflected**. The diagram below shows light being reflected in a plane mirror (flat, smooth, shiny).

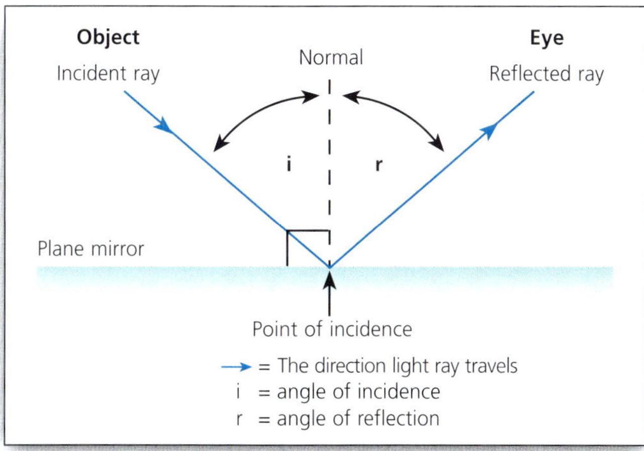

Angle of incidence = Angle of reflection

The **normal** line is perpendicular to the reflecting surface at the point of incidence. It is used to calculate the angles of incidence and reflection. The **incident ray** is the light ray travelling towards the mirror. The **reflected ray** is the light ray travelling away from the mirror.

Refraction of Light at an Interface

Light changes direction when it crosses an interface, i.e. a boundary between two transparent materials (media) of different densities, unless it meets the boundary at an angle of 90° (i.e. along the normal).

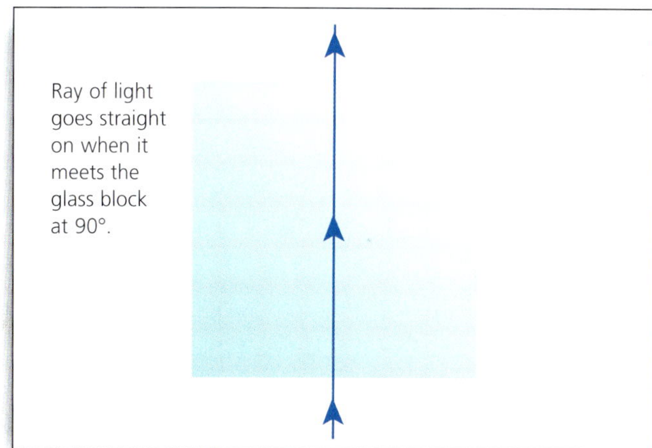

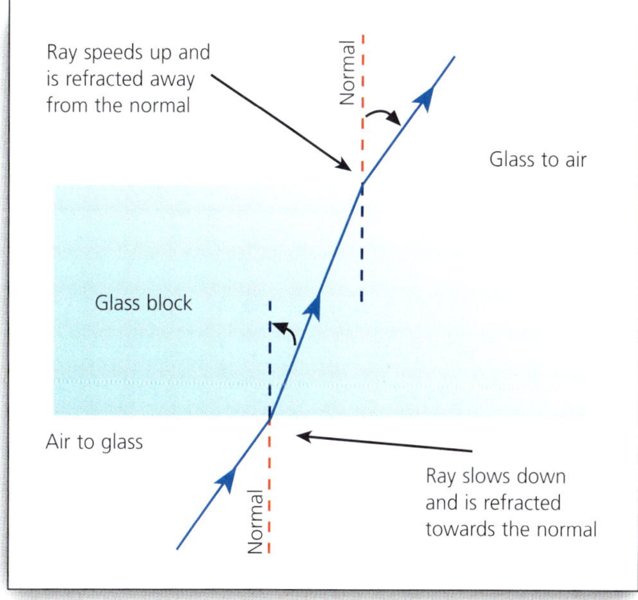

Internal Reflection

When a ray of light travels from glass, Perspex or water into air, some light is also reflected at the interface. This is called **internal reflection**.

Total internal reflection (where no light is refracted at all) occurs when the angle of incidence exceeds a certain value, called the **critical angle**. The critical angle for glass is approximately 42°.

Three possibilities are looked at below:

Angle of Incidence < Critical Angle

Most light is refracted; there is a little internal reflection.

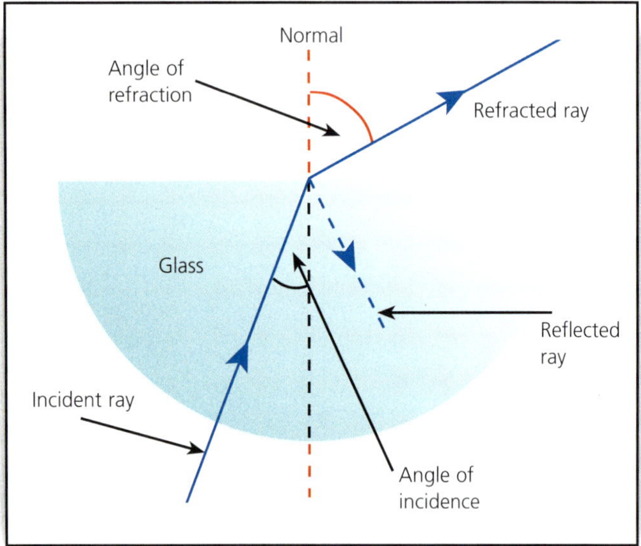

Angle of Incidence = Critical Angle

Light is refracted at 90° to the normal; there is some internal reflection.

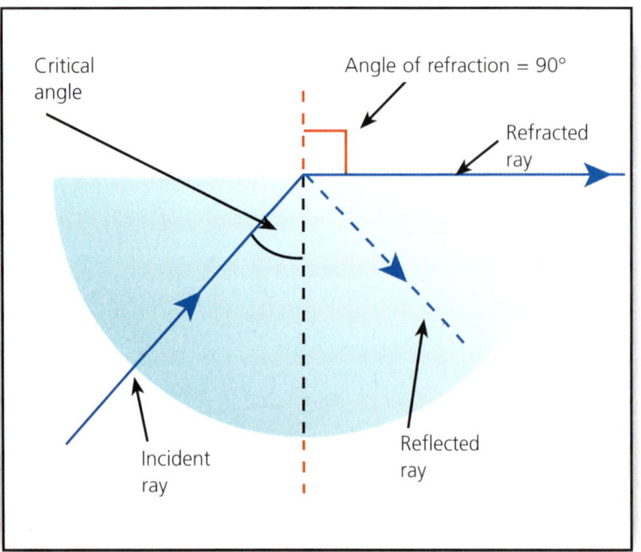

Angle of Incidence > Critical Angle

Total internal reflection; no refraction.

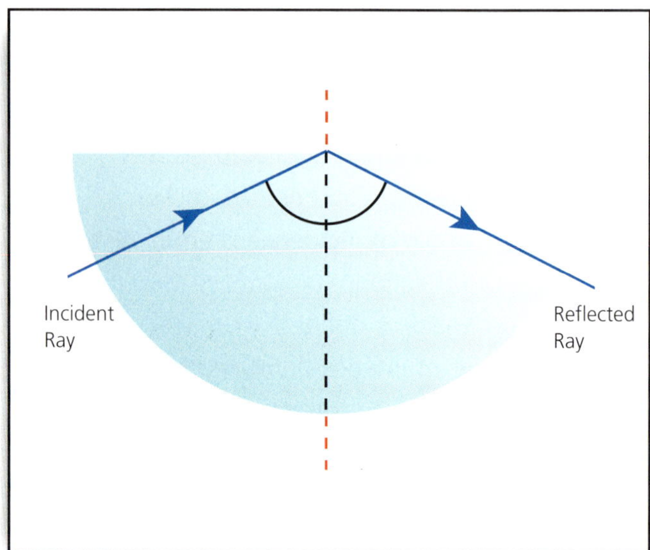

Refraction by a Prism

A triangular prism has no parallel sides. Light travelling through it is not returned to its original direction, i.e. the ray is deviated.

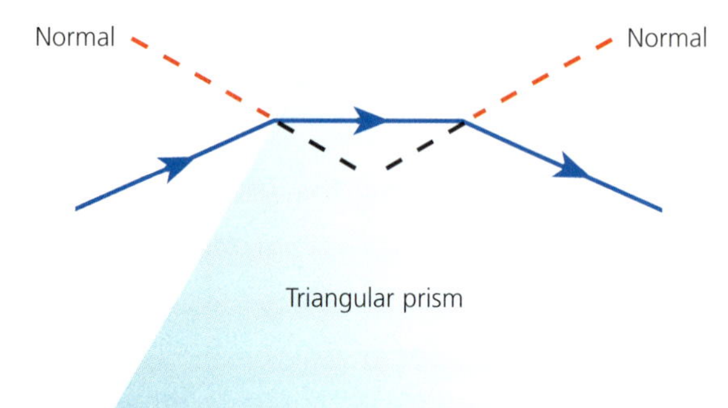

Images

The principles of reflection and refraction can be used to form **images** in optical devices (like cameras and magnifying glasses) using mirrors and lenses. An image is a representation of an object.

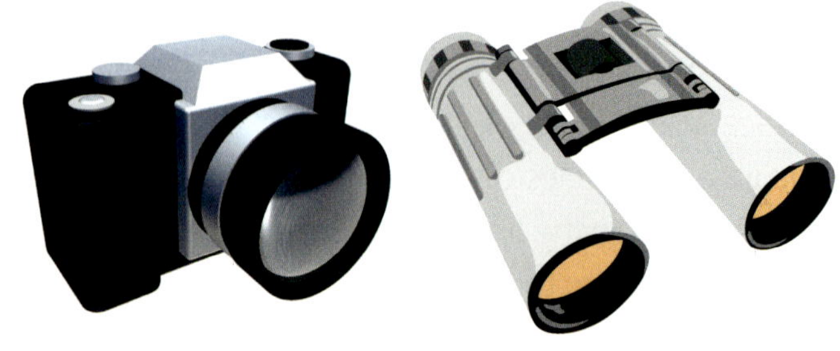

Images Produced by Mirrors

Different mirrors produce different types of images:

1 The image formed by a **plane** mirror is the same size as the object. It is upright and laterally inverted (faces the opposite way to the object).

Look at the diagram opposite. The rays of light reaching the eye appear to come directly from the image. Because the rays of light do not actually come from the image, it is described as a **virtual** image.

2 An image formed by a **convex** mirror (curving outwards) appears to be formed at a single point behind the mirror. The image is smaller than the object and is virtual and upright. This type of mirror can be used in rear-view mirrors in cars.

3 **Concave** mirrors form images inside the curve of the mirror at the point where all the rays of light converge (come together). This is called the **focus point** (F).
Concave mirrors produce different images depending on where the object is in relation to the mirror.

If the distance from the object to the mirror is less than the distance from the mirror to F, the image produced is virtual, upright and larger than the object.

If the distance from the object to the mirror is greater than the distance from the mirror to F, the image is inverted (upside down) and laterally inverted. The size of the image will vary, depending on how far away the object is from the mirror: the greater the distance, the smaller the object.

In this case, the image will also be **real**. A real image is formed when rays of light actually meet (rather than just appear to).

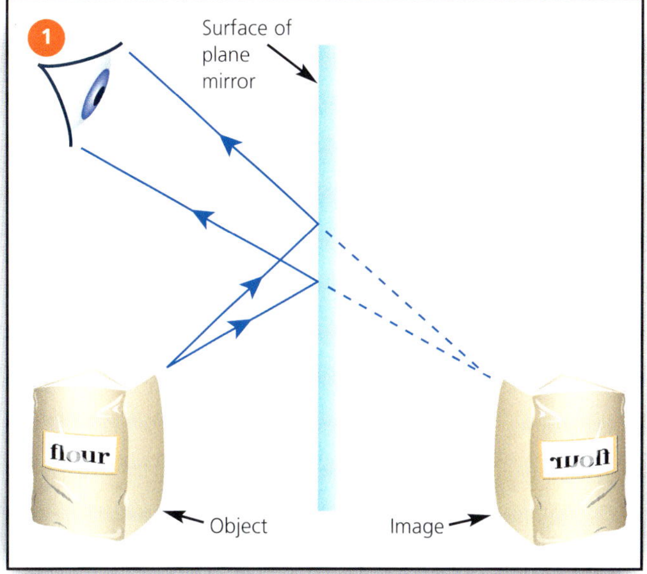

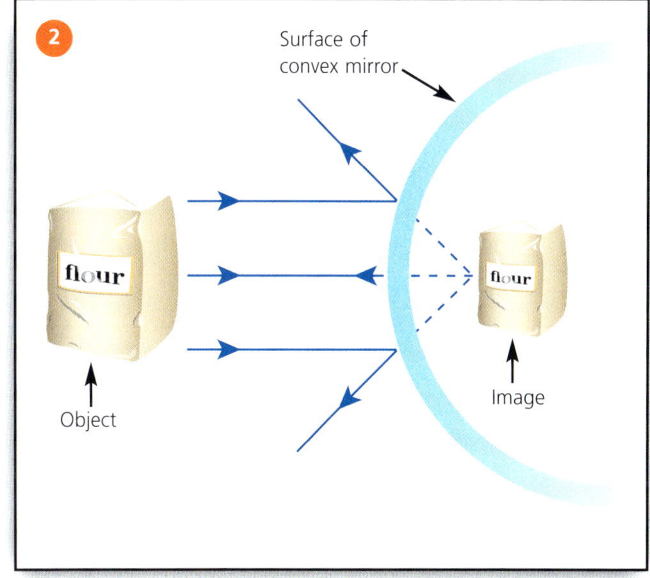

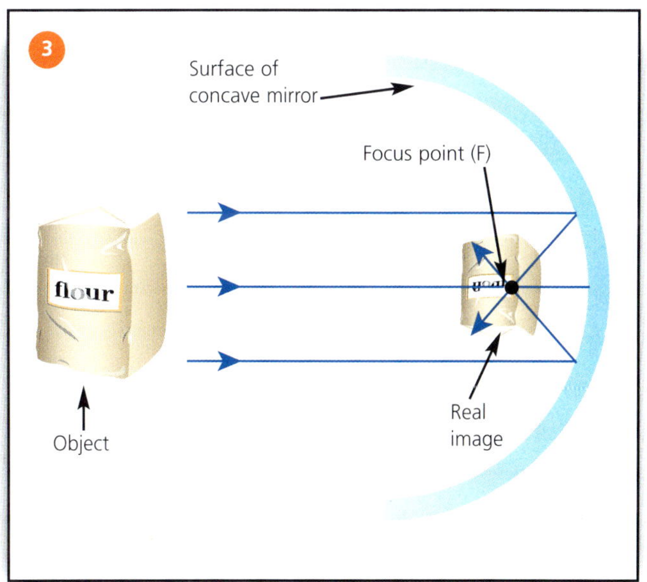

Images Produced by Lenses

A lens is a piece of transparent material which refracts light rays. There are two types of lens: **diverging** and **converging**. They have a different curvature, therefore parallel rays of light pass through them differently.

1 A diverging (concave) lens is thinnest at its centre.

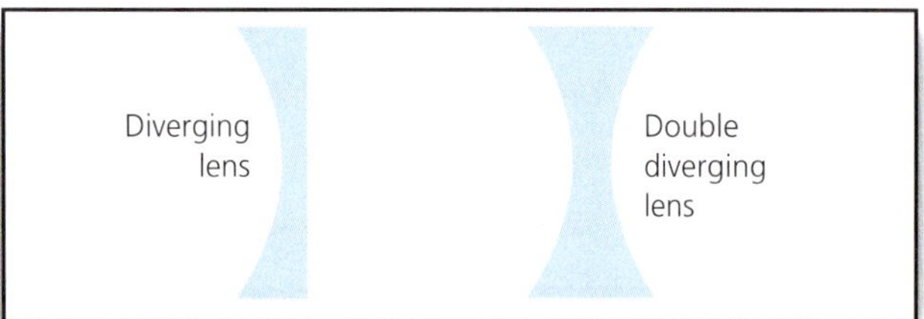

In a double concave lens, the rays of light are refracted outwards at the two curved boundaries so that they appear to come from one point, the focus (F). Only the middle ray, which meets the lens at 90°, passes straight through.

The image produced by a diverging lens is virtual and upright.

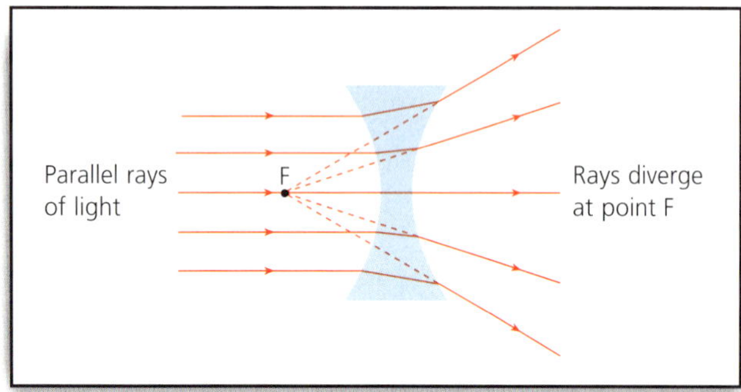

2 A converging (convex) lens is thickest at its centre.

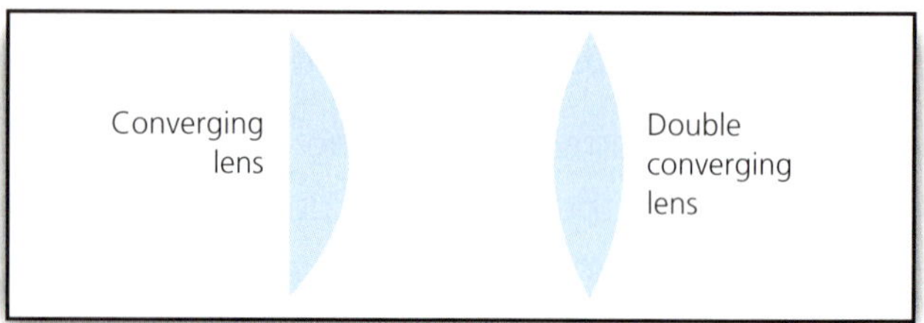

In a double convex lens, the light rays are refracted inwards at the two curved boundaries to converge (meet) at one point called the focus (F). Only the middle ray, which meets the lens at 90°, passes straight through.

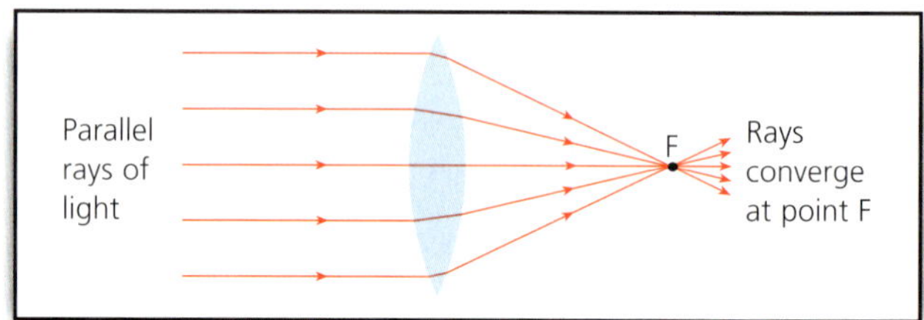

The image produced by a converging lens depends on the distance of the object from the lens.

If the distance from the object to the lens is greater than the distance from the lens to the focus point (F), it will produce a real image that is inverted and laterally inverted. This type of lens is used in cameras.

If the distance from the object to the lens is less than the distance from the lens to the focus point (F), it will produce a virtual image that is upright, enlarged and seems to be formed on the same side of the lens. This type of lens is used in magnifying glasses.

The Camera

Distant object

Rays to form image

Photographic film

Converging lens

Image

A converging lens is used in a camera to produce an image of an object on photographic film.

The image formed is smaller and nearer to the lens, compared to the object.

You need to be able to calculate the magnification produced by a lens using the formula:

$$\text{Magnification} = \frac{\text{Image height}}{\text{Object height}}$$

Example

Most cameras produce negatives that are 24mm in height (landscape). To produce photographic prints, the images on the negatives have to be increased in size using an enlarger, which contains a magnifying lens. Calculate the magnification of the lens needed to produce...

1. a small print which is 96mm in height
2. a large print which is 264mm in height.

1. Using the formula... $\frac{96}{24} = \mathbf{4}$. Therefore, to produce a small print, which is 96mm in height, a lens with a magnification of x4 is needed.
2. Using the formula... $\frac{264}{24} = \mathbf{11}$. Therefore, to produce a large print, which is 264mm in height, a lens with a magnification of x11 is needed.

You need to be able to construct ray diagrams to show the formation of images by convex and concave mirrors.

A ray diagram is used to determine the location, size, orientation and type of image formed by a mirror. To draw a diagram, first draw a horizontal axis and a convex / concave mirror. The horizontal axis should run through the centre of the mirror. Then mark up the focus points (F), one on either side of the mirror. They should both be the same distance away from the mirror. Now mark the position of the object. Two rays of light can be drawn from a point on the object.

Example 1: Concave mirrors

For concave mirrors there are two rules:

1. Any incident ray travelling parallel to the horizontal axis will reflect and pass through the focal point (F) in front of the mirror.
2. Any ray travelling through F will reflect and travel parallel to the horizontal axis in front of the mirror.

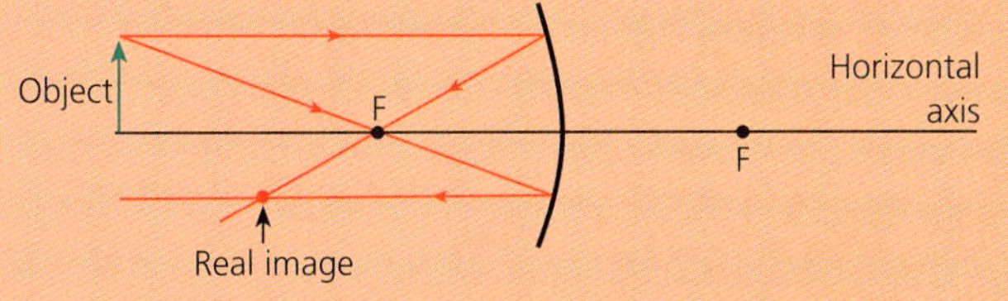

Example 2: Convex mirrors

For convex mirrors there are two rules:

1. Any incident ray travelling parallel to the principal axis will reflect in a manner that its extension will pass though the focal point behind the mirror.
2. Any incident ray travelling through the focal point in front of the mirror will reflect and travel parallel to the principal axis.

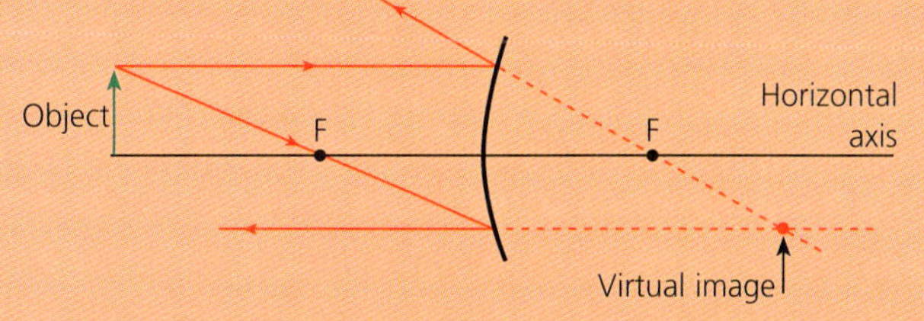

How Science Works

You need to be able to explain the use of a converging lens as a magnifying glass and construct ray diagrams to show the formation of images by diverging and converging lenses.

Ray diagrams can determine the path of light from an object to our eyes. By drawing them we can find out the location, size, orientation and type of image formed. Regardless of where the object is, the principle for drawing ray diagrams is the same.

To draw a ray diagram, first draw a horizontal axis and a double convex / concave lens. The horizontal axis should run through the centre of the lens. Mark up the focal point (F) on both sides of the lens. They should be the same distance from the centre of the lens. Now mark up 2F, again on both sides of the lens. Each 2F should be the same distance from F, as F is from the lens. Now mark the position of the object (i.e. outside 2F, at 2F, at F, etc.). There are three rays of light that can now be drawn from a point on the object.

- **Ray 1** runs parallel to the horizontal axis until it hits the lens. It will then refract through F.
- **Ray 2** goes straight through the centre of the lens and emerges from the lens undeflected.
- **Ray 3** passes through F until it hits the lens. It will then refract and travel parallel to the horizontal axis.

The image occurs at the point where these rays intersect.

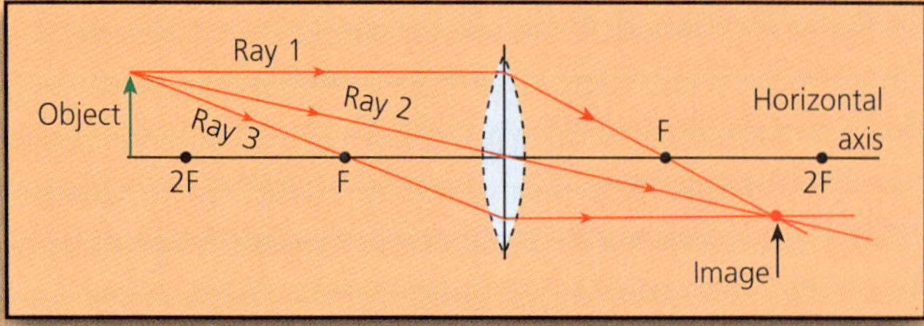

To find the location of the image you only actually need to draw two of these rays, so for the following diagrams we shall use rays 1 and 2.

Double Converging Lenses

The image produced with a converging lens depends on where the object is in relation to the focus point.

When the object is located beyond 2F, the image will be located on the other side of the lens. The image will be real, inverted and smaller. This type of lens is used in cameras.

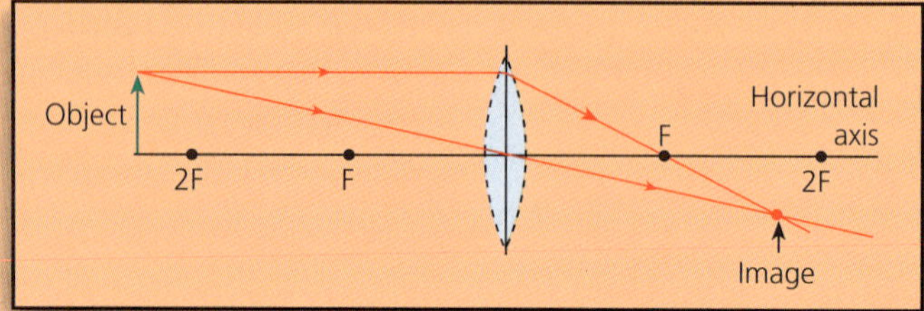

If the object is at F, the refracted rays will be parallel and will never meet. The image is formed at infinity, i.e. you will never be able to see it.

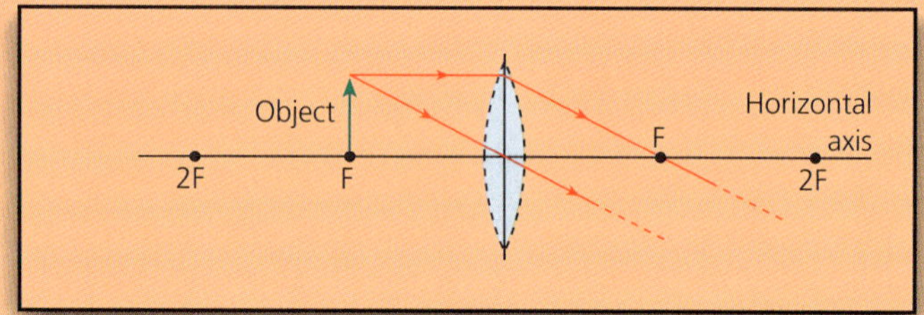

If the object is located in front of F, the light rays diverge after refracting through the lens. The image location can be found by tracing all light rays backwards until they intersect. This produces a virtual, upright and enlarged image. This is used in a magnifying glass.

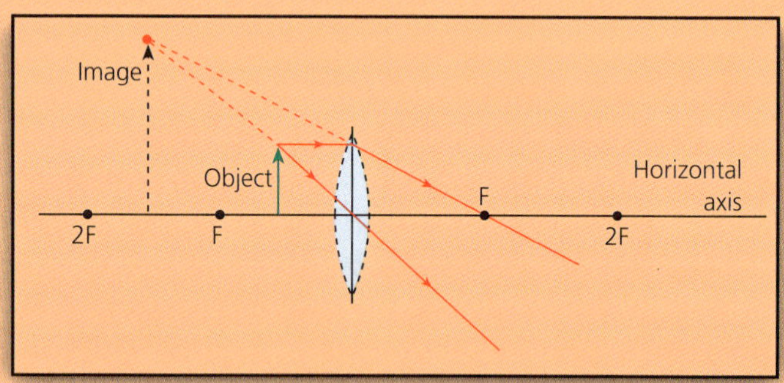

Double Diverging Lenses

The rays diverge after they are refracted. The image location can be found by tracing Ray 1 backwards until it intersects Ray 2. The image produced from a diverging lens will always be virtual and upright, regardless of the position of the object.

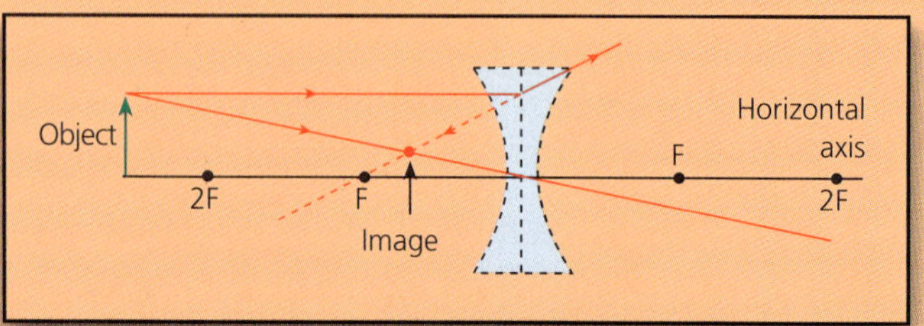

13.5

What is sound?

Sound is a mechanical vibration that can be detected by the human ear. To understand how sound works, you need to know...

- how sound travels
- how the pitch of a sound can be increased
- how the loudness of a sound can be increased.

Sound Waves

Sounds travel as waves. They are produced when something vibrates backwards and forwards. The quality of a note depends on the waveform.

Sound cannot travel through a vacuum; it **reflects** off hard surfaces to produce echoes; and is **refracted** when it passes into a different medium or substance. Sound can also be **diffracted** around buildings or land masses, so a person in the 'shadow' of a large building can still hear sounds which we might expect to be 'blocked'.

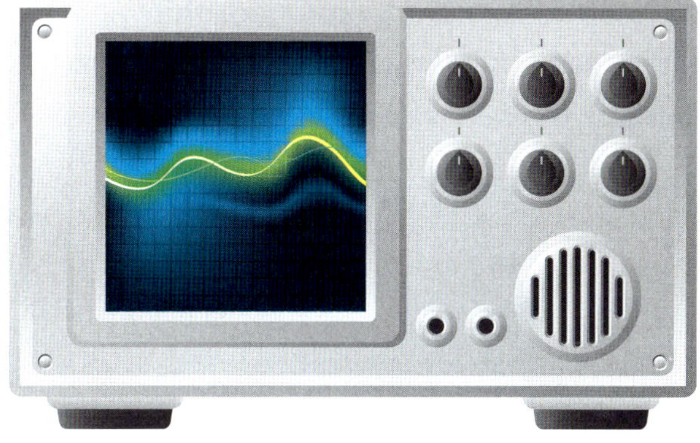

Frequency and Pitch

The frequency of a sound wave is the number of vibrations produced in one second. It is measured in hertz (Hz). Humans can hear sounds in the range of 20–20 000 Hz. The frequency affects the pitch of the sound:

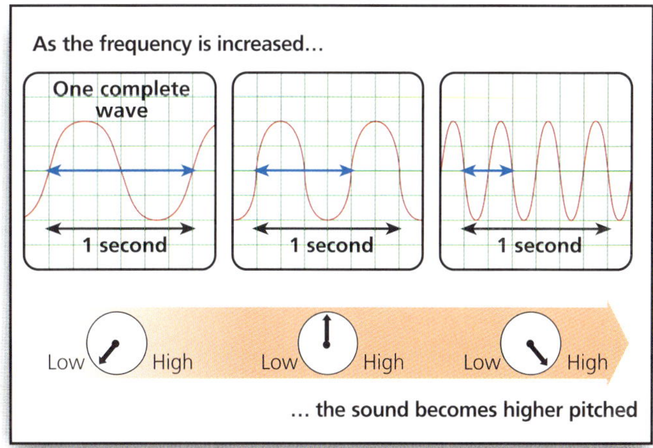

Amplitude and Loudness

Amplitude is the peak of movement of the sound wave from its rest point. The amplitude affects the loudness of the sound:

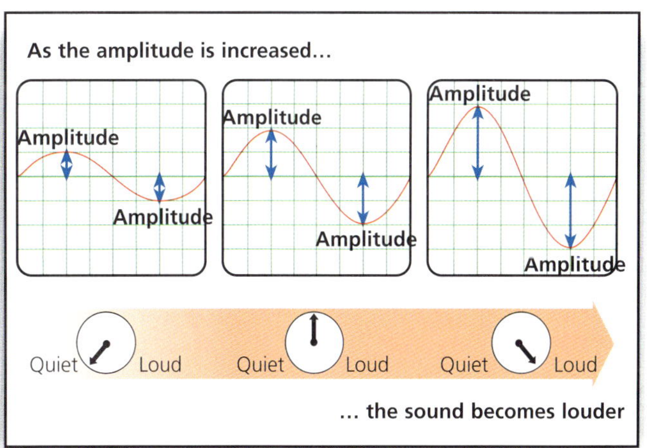

How Science Works

You need to be able to compare the amplitudes and frequencies of sounds from diagrams of oscilloscope traces.

Example

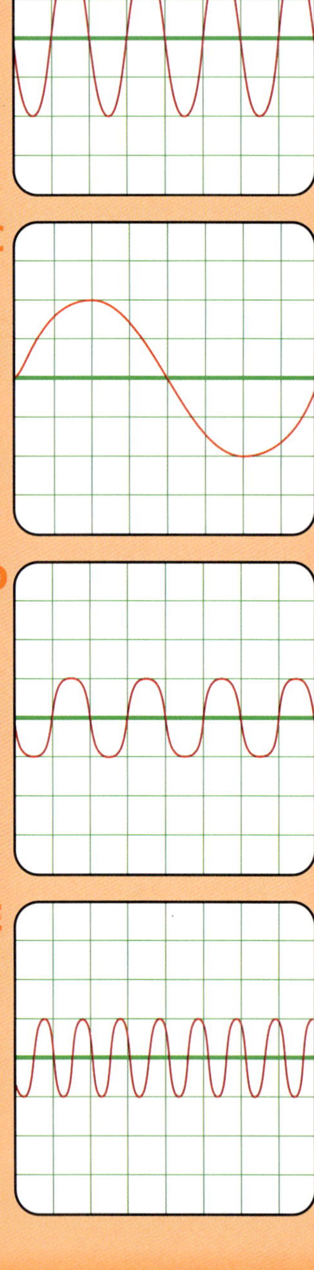

Diagrams A, B, C, D and E alongside show oscilloscope traces. Which trace shows the loudest and the lowest pitched sound? In order to answer this you need to find a trace that has a high amplitude and low frequency, so look for a trace which has the highest peak and the smallest number of waves.

First, look at the amplitude of each of the traces to decide which shows the loudest sounds.

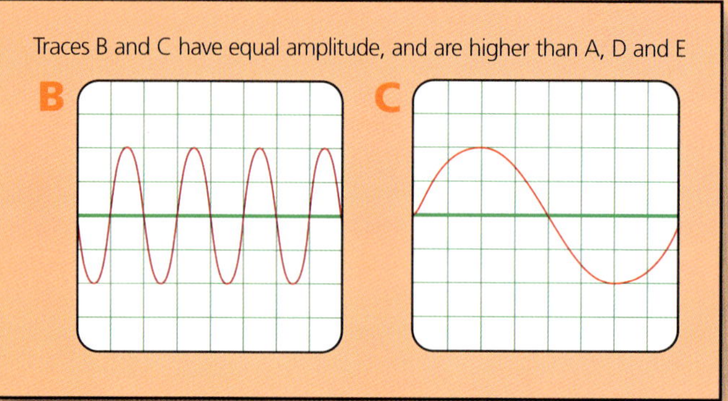

Traces B and C have equal amplitude, and are higher than A, D and E

Next, look at the frequency of each of the traces to decide which shows the lowest pitched sounds.

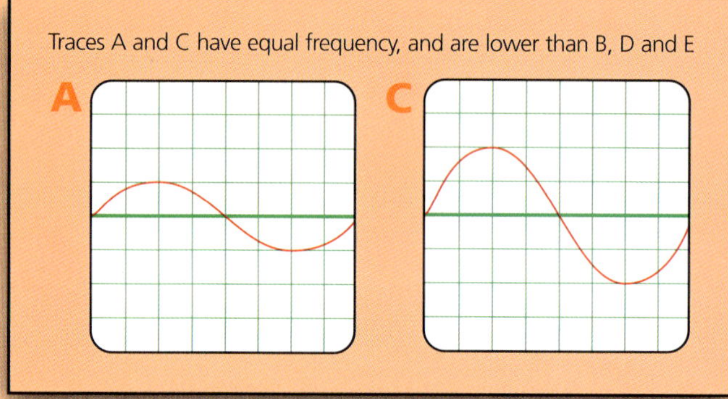

Traces A and C have equal frequency, and are lower than B, D and E

Traces D and E have neither the highest amplitude nor the lowest frequency, so you can dismiss these traces and concentrate on traces A, B and C. Traces B and C show the loudest sounds, and traces A and C show the lowest pitched sounds.

So trace C must be the loudest and lowest pitched sound (this has the highest amplitude and the lowest frequency).

C

13.6

What is ultrasound and how can it be used?

Ultrasound is sound waves that are pitched at a frequency undetectable to the human ear. To understand how it is used, you need to know...

- how ultrasound waves are produced
- what happens when ultrasound waves meet a boundary between different media
- how ultrasound can be used.

Ultrasound

Ultrasound is sound waves of frequencies greater than 20 000Hz, i.e. above the upper limit of the hearing range for humans. Electronic systems produce electrical oscillations which are used to generate the ultrasonic waves.

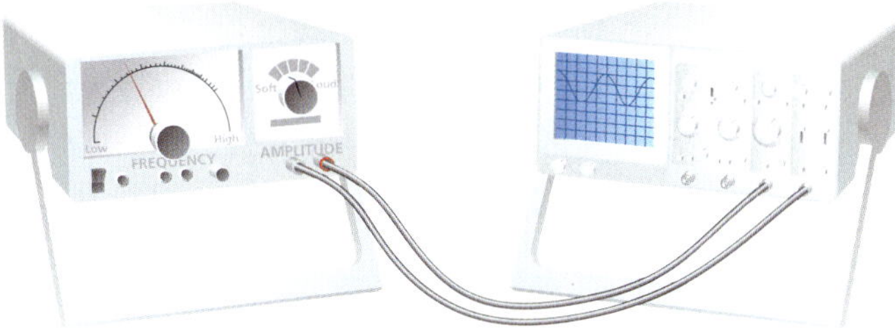

As ultrasonic waves pass from one medium or substance into another they are partly reflected at the boundary. The time taken for these reflections is a measure of how far away the boundary is. The reflected waves are usually processed to produce a visual image on a screen.

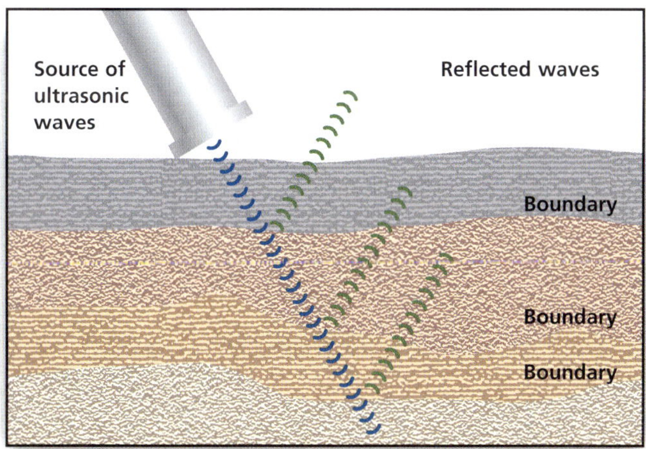

Uses

Ultrasounds can be used in many ways.

Pre-natal Scanning

This method is safe with no risk to the patient or baby.

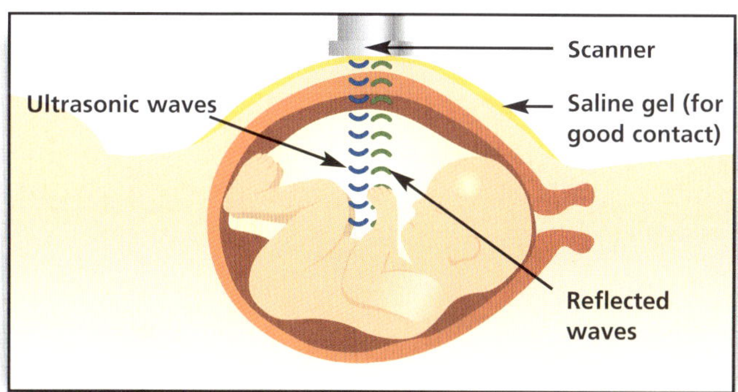

Detecting Flaws and Cracks

Some of the ultrasound waves are reflected back by the flaw or crack within the structure.

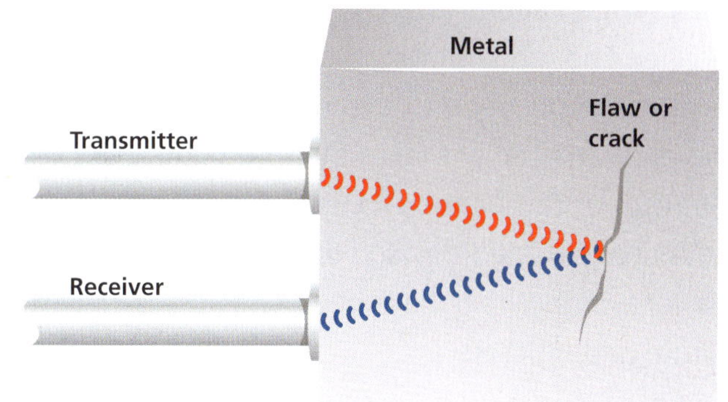

Cleaning Delicate Objects

The vibrations caused by the ultrasound waves can be used within a liquid to dislodge dirt particles from the surface of an object. Using this method means there is no danger of breakage and no need to take the object apart.

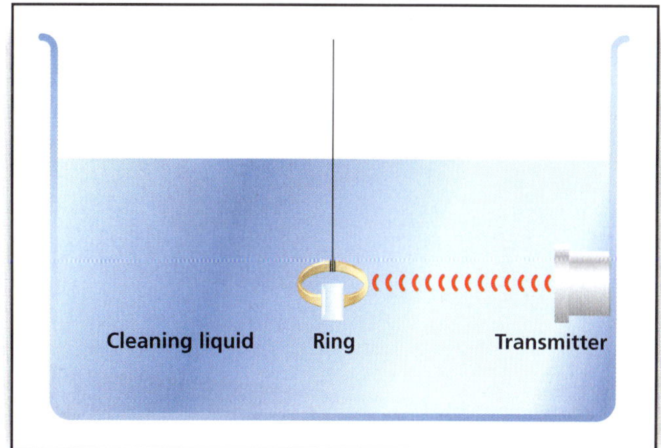

How Science Works

You need to be able to compare the amplitudes and frequencies of ultrasounds from diagrams of oscilloscope traces and determine the distance between interfaces in various media from diagrams of oscilloscope traces.

Example

Ultrasound equipment is used in foundries to test cast metal for flaws. Flaws, like cracks and bubbles of gas trapped in the metal, can dangerously weaken the castings.

The ultrasound waves are transmitted through the castings. When they meet a boundary between two substances of different densities, e.g. the other side of the metal object or a flaw in the metal, some of the waves are reflected back.

The reflected sound waves (echoes) are detected by a receiver. The longer it takes for the wave to reach the receiver the deeper into the metal it has travelled. Therefore, the time it takes them to bounce back to the receiver can be used to work out whether the waves have passed through the object to the other side or whether they have been reflected by a flaw before getting there.

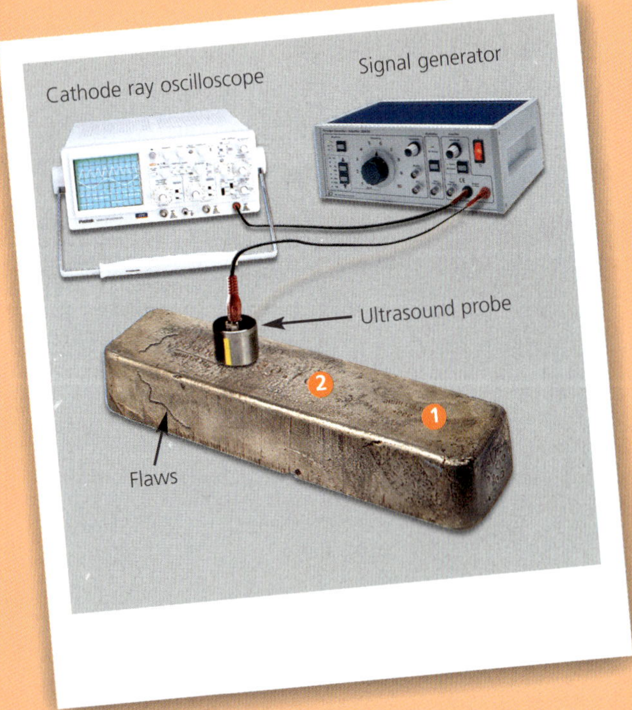

1

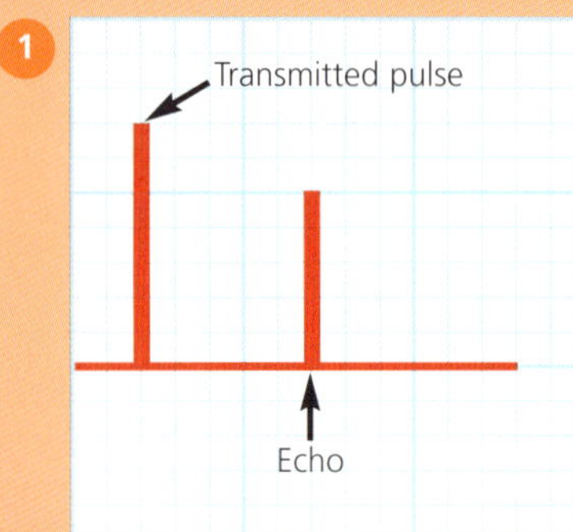

The echo has lower amplitude than the transmitted pulse, because waves spread out as they get further away from the source (i.e. amplitude and frequency decrease).

2

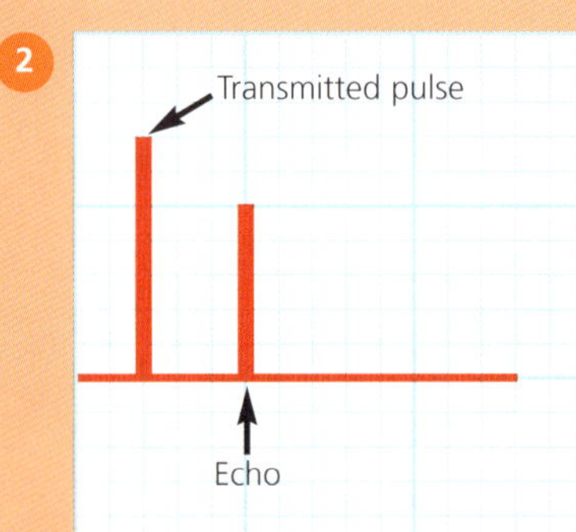

Above are traces produced at positions 1 and 2 on the diagram opposite. Trace 1 shows an echo that has travelled cleanly through the metal and been reflected at the boundary on the other side. On Trace 2, the echo is returned quicker, so it must have been reflected by a flaw.

HT Calculate the depth of the flaw if each square on the trace represents 1 microsecond (1×10^{-6} second) and the sound waves travel through the metal at 5000m/s.

Using the equation, Distance = Speed x Time…

1 Distance $= 5000\text{m/s} \times 3 \times 10^{-6}\text{s}$

(or 5000m/s x 0.000 003s)

$= 1.5 \times 10^{-2}\text{m}$ (or 0.015m)

= 1.5cm

Remember, this is the distance there and back, so the depth of the flaw in the metal is actually half this amount.

$\frac{1.5}{2} = \mathbf{0.75cm}$

The flaw is 0.75cm beneath the surface of the metal in the casting.

13.7

How can electricity be used to make things move?

Electric currents produce magnetic fields, and forces produced in magnetic fields can be used to make things move. This is called the motor effect. To understand this, you need to know...

- how a force is created
- how the size of a force can be increased
- how to reverse the direction of a force.

The Principles of The Motor Effect

In the motor effect, **current produces movement**. When a conductor (wire) carrying an electric current is placed in a magnetic field, the magnetic field formed around the wire interacts with the permanent magnetic field causing the wire to experience a force, which makes it move.

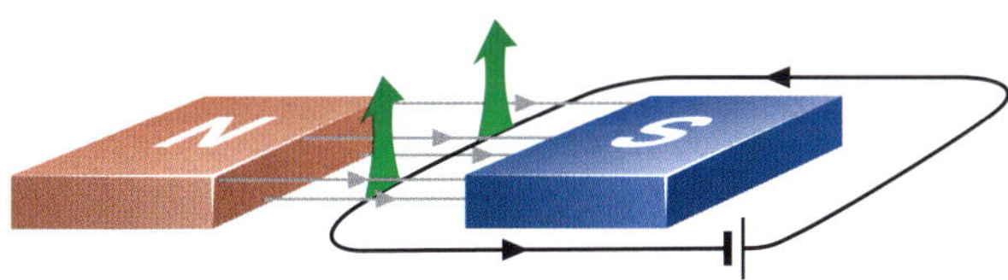

The **size** of the force on the wire can be increased by...

- increasing the size of the current (e.g. having more cells)

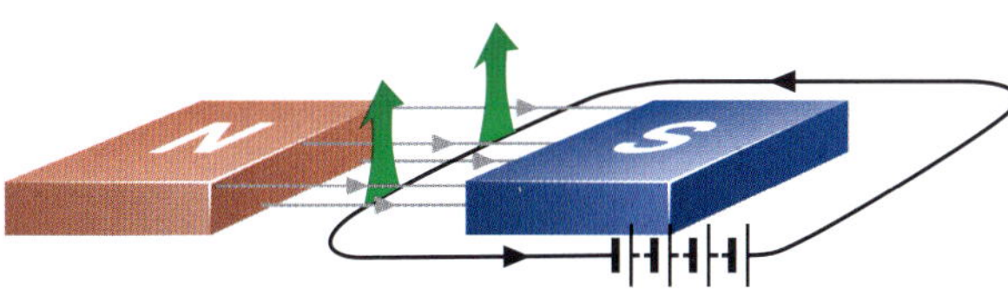

- increasing the strength of the magnetic field (e.g. having stronger magnets).

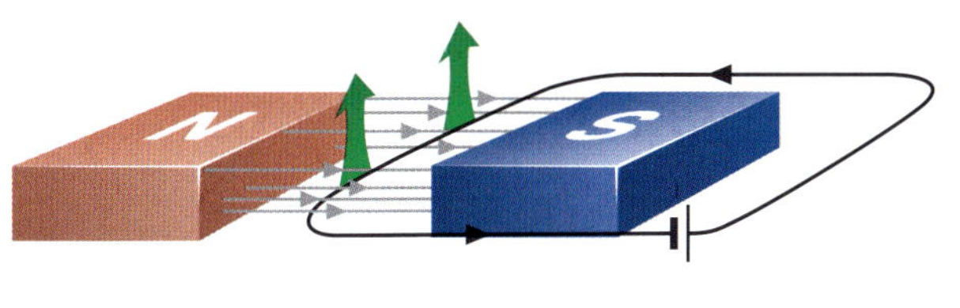

The **direction** of the force on the wire can be reversed by...

- reversing the direction of flow of the current (e.g. turning the cell around)

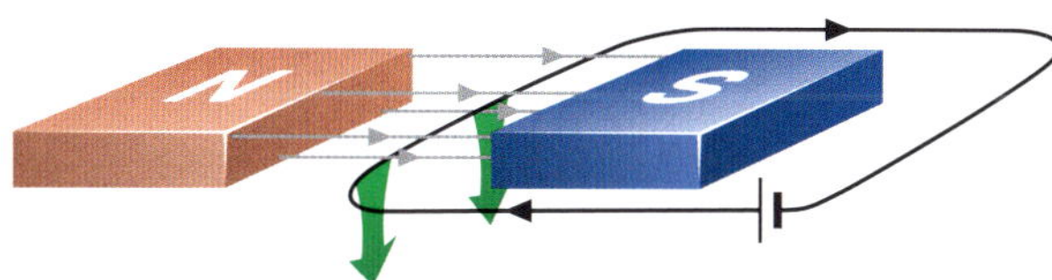

- reversing the direction of the magnetic field (e.g. swapping the magnets around).

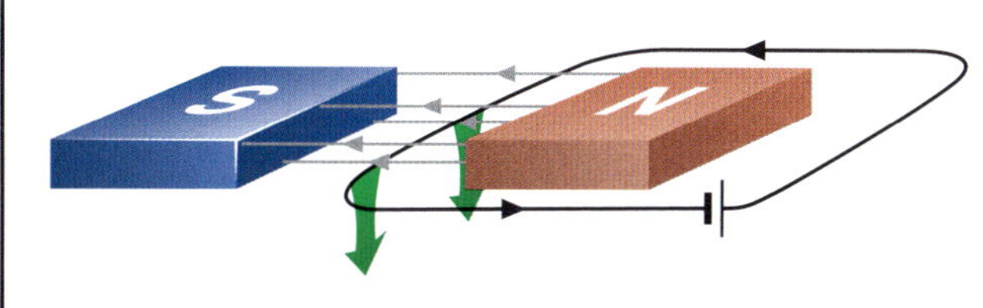

The wire will not experience a force if it is parallel to the magnetic field.

The Direct Current Motor

Electric motors rely on the principle of the motor effect. They form the basis of a vast range of electrical devices both inside and outside the home.

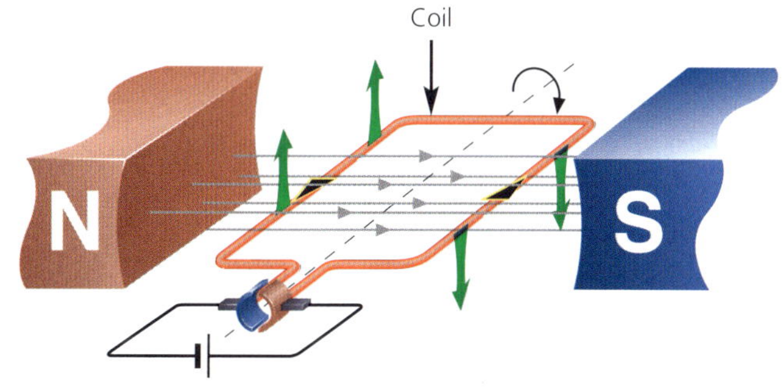

As a current flows through the coil, a magnetic field is formed around the coil, creating an electromagnet. This magnetic field interacts with the permanent magnetic field which exists between the two poles, North and South. A force acts on both sides of the coil, which rotates the coil to give us a very simple motor.

How Science Works

You need to be able to explain how the motor effect is used in simple devices.

Example

How do SPEAKERS work?

The speakers in your stereo or earpiece of your MP3 player make use of the motor effect.

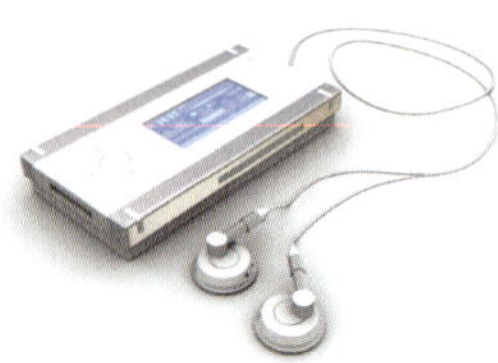

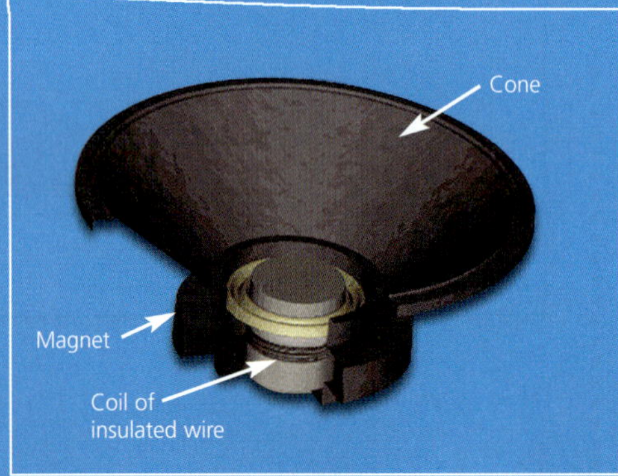

A loudspeaker is made up of the following parts:

- a permanent magnet
- a light coil of insulated wire wound on a tube
- a paper cone fixed to the coil and tube.

Firstly, an electrical signal is fed to the speaker. This signal has a varying current with a frequency that changes to match the frequency of the music.

The current then goes through the coil of insulating wire and this turns the coil into a very weak magnet. Because the current varies, the strength of the magnetic field of the coil keeps changing. This causes the force between the coil and the permanent magnet to keep changing as well.

As a result, the coil vibrates at the same frequency as the music. Because it is attached to the paper cone it moves in and out, causing vibrations which are sent through the air as sound waves.

This all occurs because a magnet and a wire carrying a current both have a magnetic field and when they try to occupy the same space a force is created between them.

13.8

How do generators work?

When an electrical conductor 'cuts' through magnetic field lines, an electrical potential difference is induced across the ends of the conductor. This is called the generator effect and is used to produce electricity. To understand this, you need to know...

- how an electrical potential difference is induced
- how the induced current can be reversed
- how the size of induced potential difference can be increased.

Electromagnetic Induction

In electromagnetic induction, **movement produces current**. If a wire or a coil of wire cuts through the lines of force of a magnetic field, or vice versa, then a potential difference is induced (produced) between the ends of the wire. If the wire is part of a complete circuit, a current will be induced.

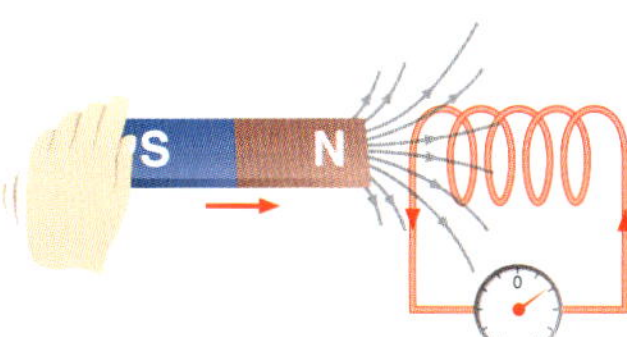

Moving the magnet into the coil induces a current in one direction. A current can be induced in the opposite direction...

- by moving the magnet out of the coil

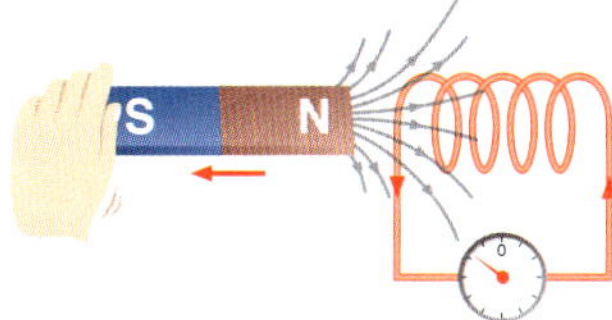

- by moving the other pole of the magnet into the coil.

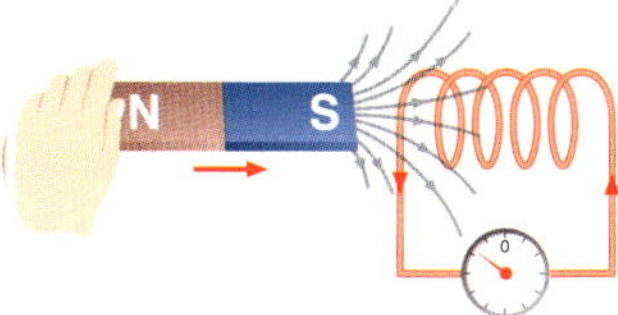

Generators use this principle for generating electricity by rotating a coil of wire within a magnetic field or rotating a magnet inside a coil.

Both of these involve a magnetic field being cut by a coil of wire, creating an induced potential difference. However, if there is no movement of magnet or coil there is no induced current.

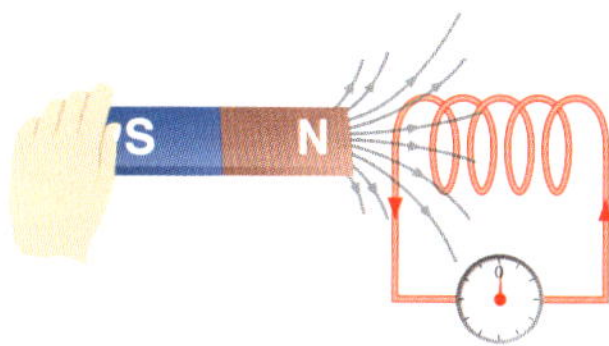

Increasing Potential Difference

The size of the induced potential difference can be increased by increasing the area of the coil. It can also be increased by...

- increasing the speed of movement of the magnet or the coil

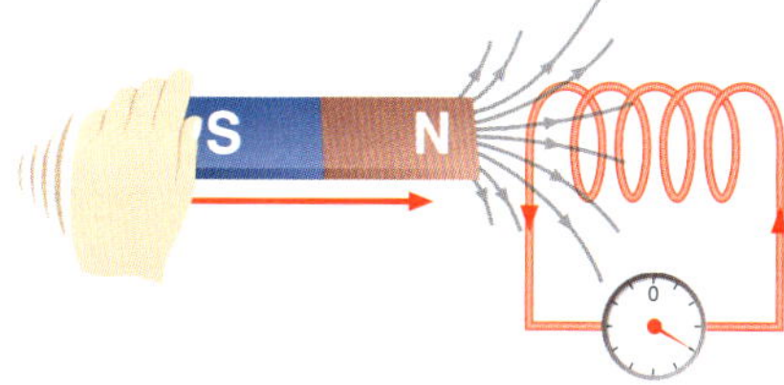

- increasing the strength of the magnetic field

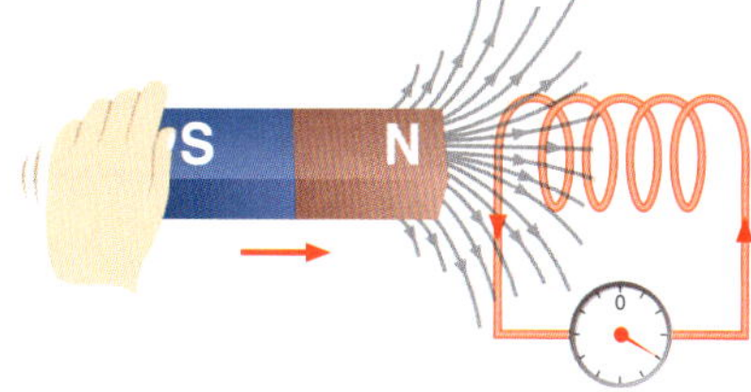

- increasing the number of turns on the coil

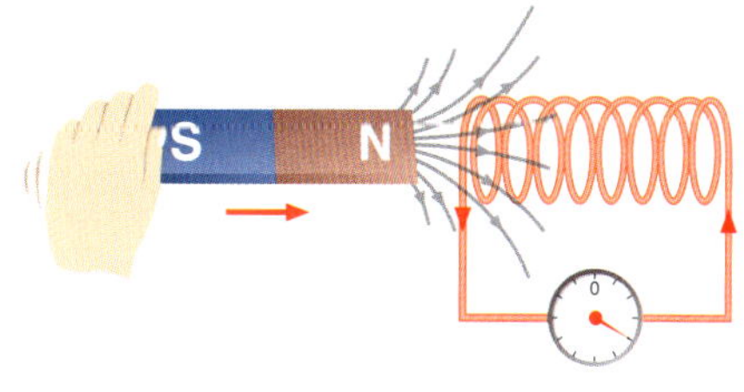

How Science Works

You need to be able to explain from a diagram how an alternating current generator works, including the purpose of slip rings and brushes.

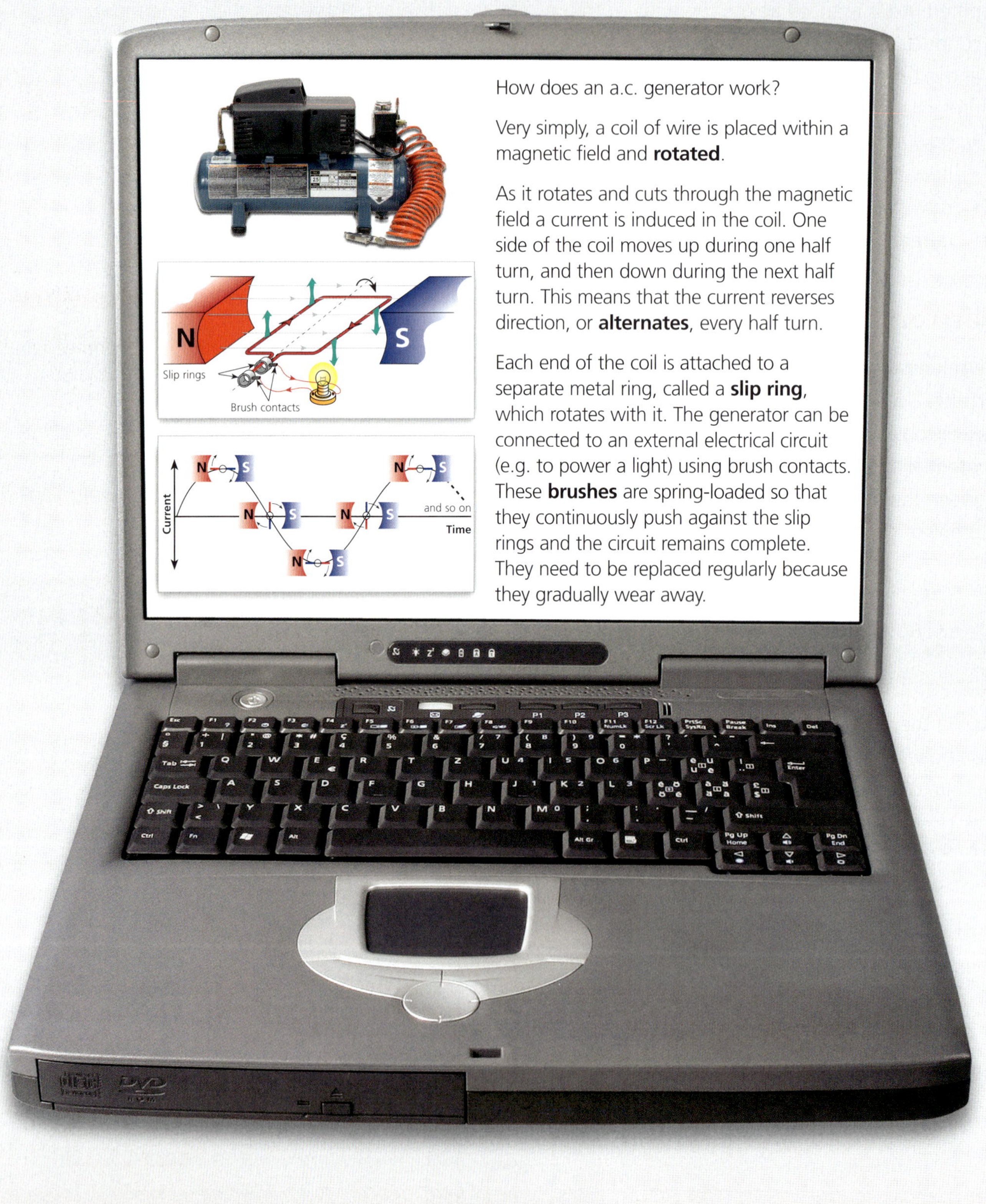

13.9

How do transformers work?

Transformers are used to increase or decrease ac potential differences. To understand how this works, you need to know...

- the basic structure of a transformer
- the difference between a step-up and step-down transformer
- how transformers are used in the National Grid.

Transformers

A transformer changes electrical energy from one potential difference to another potential difference. Transformers are used in the National Grid to ensure the efficient transmission of electricity (see page 16).

Transformers consist of two coils, called the primary and secondary coils, wrapped around a soft iron core.

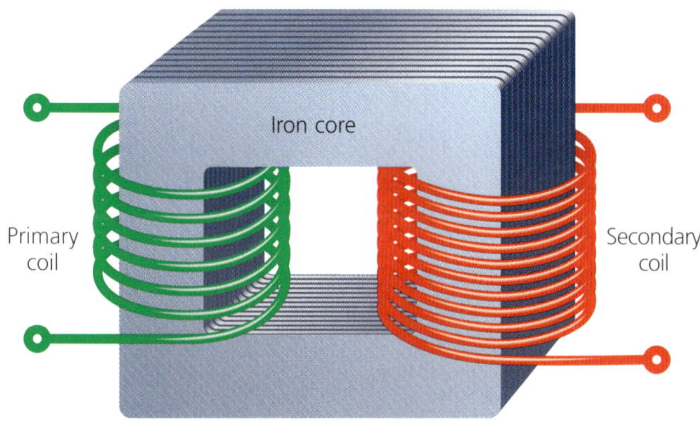

When there is an alternating potential difference across the primary coil, it causes an alternating current to flow (input). This alternating current creates a continually changing magnetic field in the iron core, which induces an alternating potential difference across the secondary coil (output). The size of the potential difference across the secondary coil depends on the relative number of turns on the primary and secondary coils.

HT

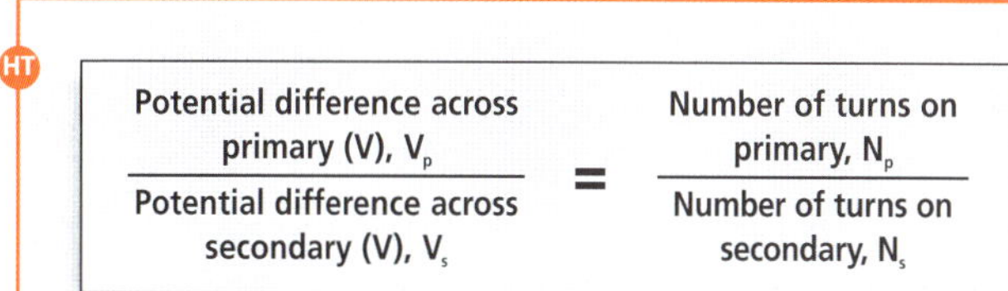

$$\frac{\text{Potential difference across primary (V), } V_p}{\text{Potential difference across secondary (V), } V_s} = \frac{\text{Number of turns on primary, } N_p}{\text{Number of turns on secondary, } N_s}$$

Example

A transformer has 200 turns on the primary coil and 800 turns on the secondary coil. If a potential difference of 230V is applied to the primary coil, what is the potential difference across the secondary coil?

Using our formula... $\frac{V_p}{V_s} = \frac{N_p}{N_s}$

$$\frac{230V}{V_s} = \frac{200}{800}$$

$$V_s = \frac{230 \times 800}{200} = \mathbf{920\ volts}$$

Or, since there are four times as many turns on the secondary coil, V_s will be four times V_p, i.e.

$$V_s = 4 \times V_p = 4 \times 230V = \mathbf{920V}$$

Step-Up and Step-Down Transformers

Step-Up Transformer

In a step-up transformer there are more turns in the secondary coil than the primary coil, so the potential difference or voltage leaving the secondary coil is **greater** than that of the primary coil.

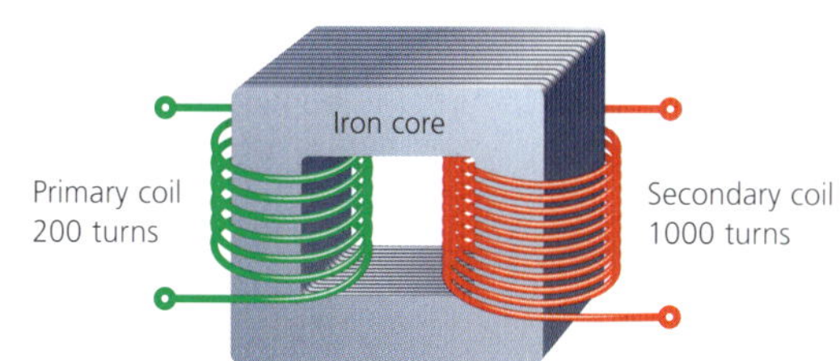

Step-Down Transformer

In a step-down transformer there are fewer turns in the secondary coil than the primary coil, so the potential difference or voltage leaving the secondary coil is **less** than that of the primary coil.

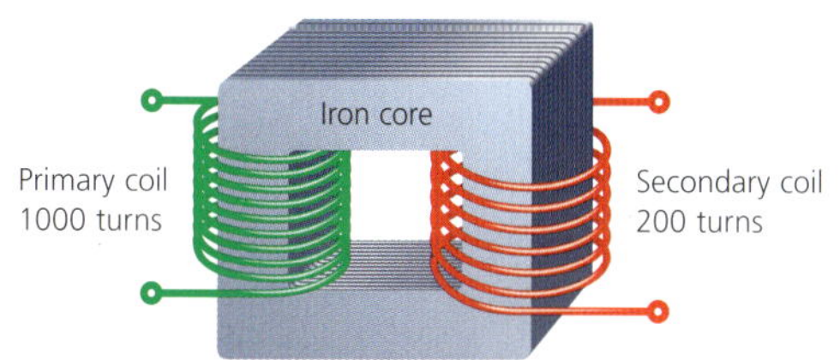

How Science Works

You need to be able to determine which type of transformer should be used for a particular application.

There are two basic types of transformer: step-up and step-down transformers. They are used in many ways as part of everyday life to increase or decrease the potential difference of an appliance. It is important that we know which type of transformer to use.

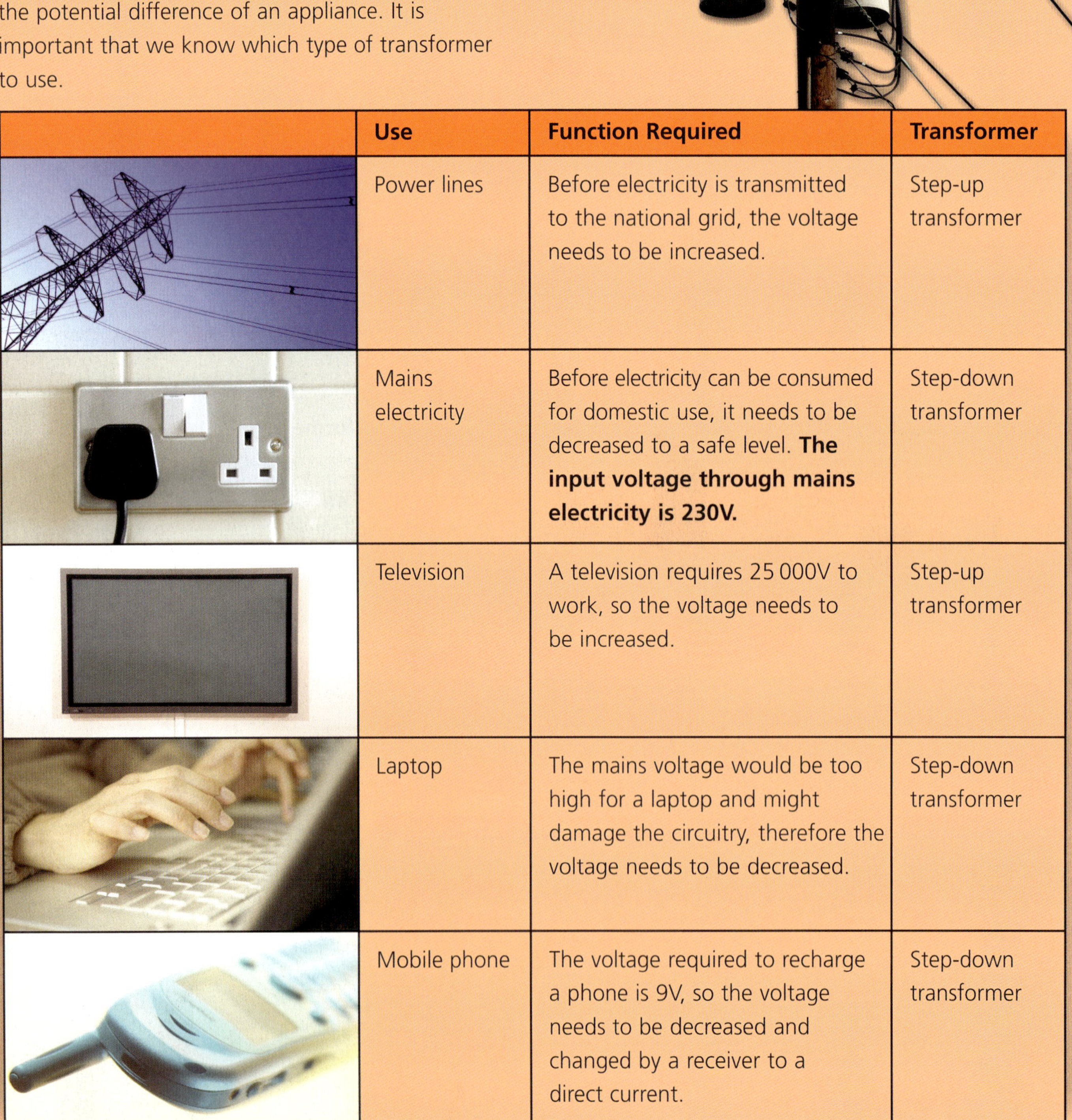

	Use	Function Required	Transformer
	Power lines	Before electricity is transmitted to the national grid, the voltage needs to be increased.	Step-up transformer
	Mains electricity	Before electricity can be consumed for domestic use, it needs to be decreased to a safe level. **The input voltage through mains electricity is 230V.**	Step-down transformer
	Television	A television requires 25 000V to work, so the voltage needs to be increased.	Step-up transformer
	Laptop	The mains voltage would be too high for a laptop and might damage the circuitry, therefore the voltage needs to be decreased.	Step-down transformer
	Mobile phone	The voltage required to recharge a phone is 9V, so the voltage needs to be decreased and changed by a receiver to a direct current.	Step-down transformer

13.10

What is the life history of stars?

Stars like the Sun have a very long, stable period. Astronomers believe that gravitational forces are responsible for this, and for the formation of galaxies. To understand this, you need to know...

- what the Universe contains
- how a star remains stable
- how a stars forms, its life cycle, and what happens when it explodes.

Formation of Stars

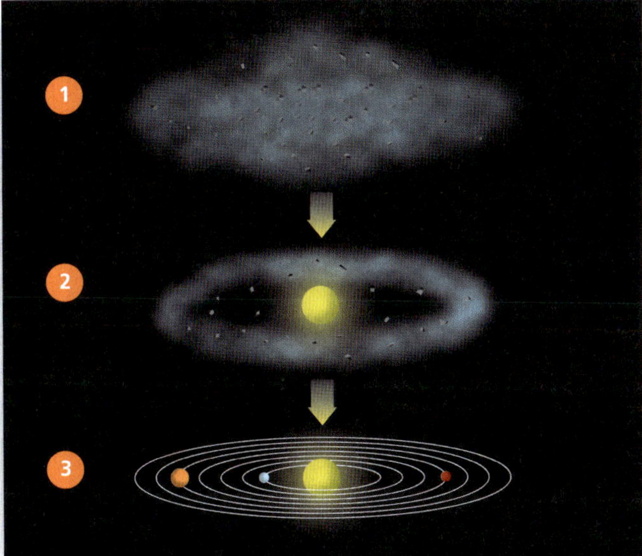

1 Gravitational attraction pulls clouds of dust, rock and gas (called nebulae) together.

2 As this mass comes together it creates heat. Eventually it becomes hot enough for hydrogen to fuse to form helium and a star is formed. This nuclear fusion releases massive amounts of energy and produces all naturally occurring elements.

3 Smaller masses may also be formed and be attracted by larger masses to become planets.

Stars use hydrogen as their source, which means they can release energy for billions of years. Our Sun is believed to be 5 billion years old and only half-way through its life. It is made up of approximately 74% hydrogen and 24% helium, with traces of heavier elements.

Our Galaxy and the Universe

Our Sun is one of the many billions of stars in our galaxy, known as the **Milky Way**. The stars in a galaxy are often millions of times further apart than the planets in the Solar System.

The stars in the night sky stay in fixed patterns (called constellations). Many of these have famous names because of their shapes, e.g. the plough.

Planets visible to the naked eye look very much like stars because of the light they reflect. However, unlike stars, they move very slowly across the night sky and therefore change their positions relative to the constellations.

The Milky Way is one galaxy in the **Universe**. The Universe is made up of billions of galaxies. Galaxies are often millions of times further apart than the stars within a galaxy.

The Life Cycle of a Star

A star remains stable during its life period due to the balance of two forces – the force of gravity pulling the star inwards is balanced by huge temperatures (radiation pressure) within the star acting outwards.

Towards the end of the star's life, two different processes may occur depending on the mass of the star:

1. A star the size of our Sun will expand to become a red giant. The red giant then cools down and will eventually collapse under its own gravity to become a white dwarf which has a density millions of times greater than any matter on Earth.

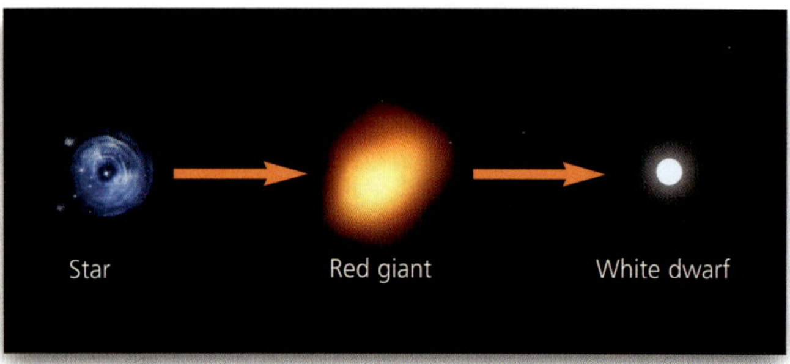

2. Stars at least four times bigger than our Sun can expand enormously to become red supergiants. The red supergiant then rapidly shrinks and explodes, releasing massive amounts of energy, dust and gas into space. This is called a supernova.

- A medium-sized star, (ten times bigger than our Sun) can then form a neutron star. This is the core of the star that remains after the explosion.

  A neutron star is made only of neutrons and is very dense. A cupful of this matter could have a mass greater than 15 000 million tonnes!

- Large stars (greater than ten times the size of our Sun) can leave behind black holes, where the matter is so dense and the gravitational field so strong that nothing can escape from it – not even light or other forms of electromagnetic radiation.

  Black holes can only be observed indirectly through their effects on their surroundings, e.g. the X-rays emitted when gases from a nearby star spiral into a black hole.

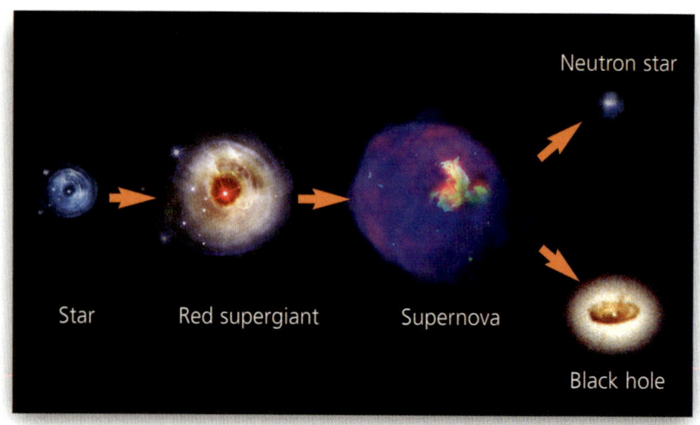

HT

Recycling Stellar Material

Stars need hydrogen as a fuel to undergo nuclear fusion, which produces helium as a product.

However, during fusion, hydrogen and helium can also fuse together to produce nuclei of heavier elements; heavier stars can fuse elements all the way up to iron.

As a star comes to the end of its life and explodes (a supernova) all of its elements are distributed throughout the Universe. This means that a large variety of different elements are circulated in the Universe, not just hydrogen.

These elements can be recycled in the formation of new stars or planets. Atoms of heavier elements are present in the inner planets of the **Solar System** which leads us to believe that the Solar System was formed from the material produced when earlier stars exploded.

Example Questions

For Unit 3, you will have to complete one written paper with structured questions.

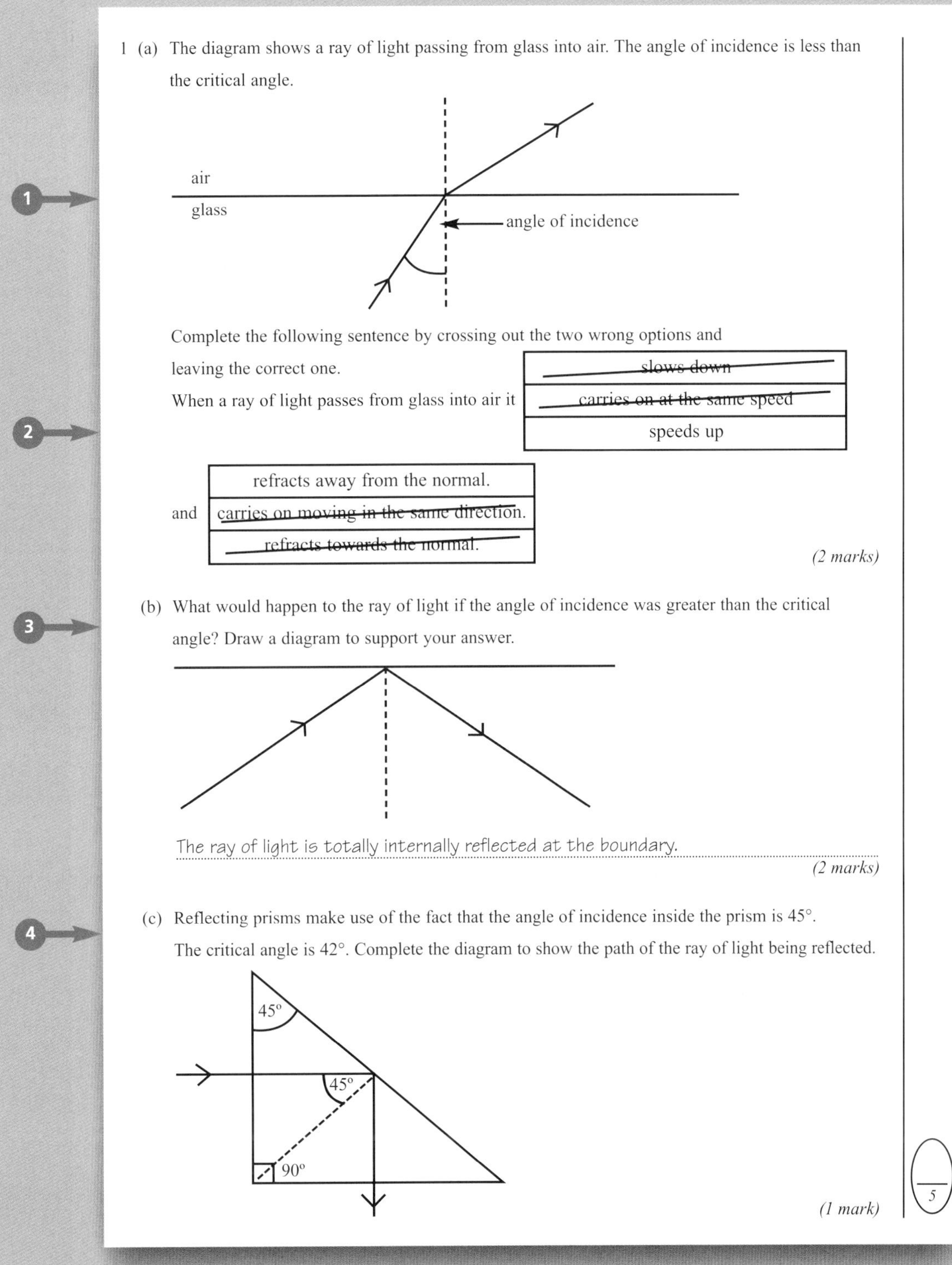

1 Look closely at any diagrams to make sure you understand what they show before answering any questions.

2 Even if you cannot remember the rules of refraction, you should be able to deduce the answer to this question from the diagram.

3 When the angle of incidence is greater than the critical angle there is always total internal reflection. The exact size of the angle in your drawing does not matter, as long as it shows this.

4 The angle of reflection is always equal to the angle of incidence. Use a ruler and make sure your line is clear and accurate.

Key Words

Alternating current – a current that changes direction
Amplitude – the maximum height of a wave
Axis – the centre around which something rotates
Centripetal force – the inward force on an object causing it to move in a circular path
Concave mirror – curves inwards
Converging lens (convex) – a lens that causes light rays passing through it to meet at a point
Convex mirror – curves outwards
Direct Current – a current that flows in only one direction
Diverging lens (concave) – a lens that causes light rays passing through it to be spread out
Ellipse – a squashed circle shape
Force – pushing or pulling action which causes a body to move, accelerate or change direction
Frequency – the number of waves produced within a given time period
Geostationary – an orbit in which a satellite is always in the same position with respect to the rotating Earth
Gravity – the force that causes objects to fall to Earth
Induced – produced
Induction – an electromagnetic force generated in an electric circuit by varying the current
Inverted – upside down
Laterally inverted – back-to-front (i.e. left side is on the right; right side is on the left)
Mass – the quantity of matter in a body
Moment – a turning force
Normal – the line which is at right angles to a reflecting / refracting surface at the point of incidence
Orbit – the curved path of an object that is moving around another object
Perpendicular – a straight line at right angles to another line
Pitch – the frequency of vibration, how high or low a sound is, changes with frequency
Pivot – an axis consisting of a short shaft that supports something that turns
Plumbline – a device used to produce a vertical line between an instrument and the reference point over which it is set
Prism – a triangular-shaped piece of glass used to deviate a ray of light
Radius – a straight line between the centre and circumference of a circle
Real image – an image produced by rays of light meeting at a point (can be projected onto a screen)
Reflection – a wave (light or sound) that is thrown back from a surface
Refraction – the change in direction of a wave as it passes from one medium to another
Stability – staying in a steady position, not falling or toppling over
Transformer – an electrical device used to change the voltage of an alternating current
Ultrasound – a sound with a frequency too high to be detected by the human ear
Virtual image – an image produced where rays of light only *appear* to meet
Weight – the vertical force exerted by a mass as a result of gravity

How Science Works Key Words

Here are the words that might be used in your exam, with a definition so you know exactly what you are being asked.

Accuracy – how correct or exact something is. The more times you repeat an experiment, the closer the average value (mean) of the results will be to the true value.

Analyse – look at in detail

Apply – relate to, put to practical use

Calculate – work out

Consider – think about

Construct – make, put together

Contrast – look at the differences between

Describe – put into words

Determine – decide, conclude

Discuss – talk about

Evaluate – determine the worth of

Evidence – results of an experiment or facts that you can use to prove or disprove a theory

Explain – put into words

Fair test – a test where conditions are controlled so no factors other than the one you are changing / controlling have an effect on what is being measured

Impact (social, economic, environmental) – an effect

Informed judgements – a balanced view based on information

Interpret – explain the meaning of

Precision – exactness, only a small spread / range of results

Predict – make a good guess at what you expect to happen

Recognise – notice, accept or be aware of

Relate – make a connection to something (like a real life situation or other experiments, etc.)

Reliability – dependability of the results, based on how accurate the measuring instruments are

Sketch – a drawing

Suggest reasons for – think of possible reasons for

Theory – an idea about what will happen

Variables – something that changes during the course of an investigation

Independent variable – the variable you change and have control over

Dependent variable – the variable (output) you measure

Notes

Acknowledgements

The author and publisher would like to thank everyone who has contributed to this book:

p.3 ©iStockphoto.com / Andrei Tchernov
p.5 ©iStockphoto.com / Audrey Roorda
p.6 ©iStockphoto.com / Todd Smith
p.7 ©iStockphoto.com / James Antrim
p.8 ©iStockphoto.com
p.10 ©iStockphoto.com
p.15 ©iStockphoto.com / Michael Finch
p.18 Used with kind permission from Hudson Reed
p.23 ©iStockphoto.com / Larry Manire
p.28 ©iStockphoto.com / Marc Dietrich
p.28 ©iStockphoto.com / Vallentin Vassileff
p.37 ©NASA
p.32 ©iStockphoto.com
p.33 ©iStockphoto.com / Mack Reed
p.43 ©iStockphoto.com / Nigel Silcock
p.50 ©iStockphoto.com / Stijn Peeters
p.54 ©iStockphoto.com / Linda Shannon
p.54 ©iStockphoto.com / Peter van Leyen
p.54 ©iStockphoto.com / Antonio Ovejero Diaz
p.57 ©iStockphoto.com / Benson Trent
p.57 ©iStockphoto.com / Christoph Ermel
p.57 ©iStockphoto.com / Andrew Howe
p.58 ©iStockphoto.com / Glenn Slingsby
p.58 ©iStockphoto.com / Luis Carlos Torres
p.58 ©iStockphoto.com / Gilles Glod
p.65 ©iStockphoto.com / Paul Cowan
p.68 ©iStockphoto.com / Sim Kay Seng
p.80 ©NASA
p.80 ©iStockphoto.com / Mark Evans
p.82 ©iStockphoto.com / Octavian Babusi
p.87 ©iStockphoto.com
p.90 ©iStockphoto.com / Shane Thompson
p.96 ©iStockphoto.com / Chris Schmelke
p.96 ©iStockphoto.com / Joseph Jean Rolland Dubé
p.96 ©iStockphoto.com / René Mansi
p.98 ©NASA

ISBN: 978-1-905129-51-5

Published by Lonsdale, a division of Huveaux Plc.

Author: Andrew Catterall
Project Editor: Charlotte Christensen
Cover and concept design: Sarah Duxbury
Designers: Richard Arundale, Ian Wrigley and Sarah Duxbury

About the Author

Andrew Catterall worked as a science teacher, specialising in physics, for 10 years before becoming a science consultant for an LEA. In his current role he works closely with the exam boards and has an excellent understanding of the new science specifications, which he is helping to implement in local schools.

Index